Practical Landscape Gardening

Robert B. Cridland

APPLEWOOD BOOKS
Bedford, Massachusetts

Practical Landscape Gardening
was originally published in

1922

9781429012980

Thank you for purchasing an Applewood book.
Applewood reprints America's lively classics—
books from the past that are still of interest
to the modern reader.
For a free copy of a catalog of our
bestselling books, write to us at:
Applewood Books
Box 365
Bedford, MA 01730
or visit us on the web at:
awb.com

Prepared for publishing by HP

THIS BOOK IS DEDICATED
BY THE AUTHOR TO

Joseph Meehan
EMINENT HORTICULTURIST
ADVISER AND FRIEND

JOSEPH MEEHAN

Practical Landscape Gardening

THE IMPORTANCE OF CAREFUL PLANNING
LOCATING THE HOUSE—ARRANGEMENT
OF WALKS AND DRIVES—CONSTRUCTION
OF WALKS AND DRIVES—LAWNS AND
TERRACES—HOW TO PLANT A PROPERTY
LAYING OUT A FLOWER GARDEN—ARCHI-
TECTURAL FEATURES OF THE GARDEN
ROSE GARDENS AND HARDY BORDERS
WILD GARDENS AND ROCK GARDENS
PLANTING PLANS AND PLANTING LISTS

BY

ROBERT B. CRIDLAND

New York
A. T. DE LA MARE COMPANY, INC.
1922

FOREWORD

This book is the outcome of a series of articles on Landscape Gardening which appeared periodically in THE FLORISTS' EXCHANGE. At the suggestion of the publisher these articles have been augmented, new subjects added, and the whole more thoroughly illustrated than was possible in the limited space of a magazine treatise.

The book is designed to appeal, in particular, to that large body of suburban home owners who have moderate sized properties susceptible of artistic arrangement and beautification.

It is not possible for the majority of men and women to give a sufficient amount of time to the study of design, horticulture and gardening, in order to treat their individual properties in a practical and artistic manner, and although nearly every one possesses the sense of taste to the extent of appreciating the difference between that which is pleasing and that which is crude or grotesque in the completed subject, very few have the time, imagination and constructive power necessary to formulate a design which will represent fully the capabilities of their own grounds, whether it be a small plot or an estate of some acres.

To assist all who are interested in the artistic development of their home surroundings it has been the author's aim in this book to set forth, in a clear and logical way, the basic principles which will bring about the most desirable environment, from a gardening standpoint, of the moderate sized city lot or the suburban estate, however limited that may be.

The text has been made as brief as possible to give more space than usual to photographic illustrations, sketches and plans, so that each subject treated may be more readily understood and applied.

Long lists of trees, shrubs, and flowers have been omitted except in those instances where planting plans are shown, accompanied by planting keys. In preparing these planting keys the type of plant necessary to secure the best effect has been considered, rather than individual varieties, and these keys are therefore subject to modification so as to suit existing conditions.

While the initial intention of the articles was to assist those engaged in gardening as a business, it is the desire of the author that all who take pleasure in the art of gardening may find in this book some additional incentive to attain that which is beautiful in landscape design.

I wish to gratefully acknowledge the valuable assistance rendered by Mr. Stanley V. Wilcox and Mr. A. T. De La Mare in the arrangement of this book.

ROBERT B. CRIDLAND.

Philadelphia, May 9, 1916.

PUBLISHERS' NOTE TO SECOND EDITION

Expecting that Mr. Robt. B. Cridland's book would be well received on account of the thorough manner in which he had covered his subject, we printed a much larger first edition than is usual with works of this character.

So great, however, has been the demand, so successful the book, that in less than eighteen months a second edition has been called for. The work in its text matter and illustrations could not easily be improved, therefore few changes have been made, with the exception of the addition of five more planting plans and keys covering moderate sized properties.

A. T. DE LA MARE CO. INC.

New York, January 15, 1918.

PUBLISHERS' NOTE TO SECOND EDITION, THIRD PRINTING

To publish a book the contents of which make for the happiness, contentment and welfare of our citizens, and to have that book appreciated as has been the case with this one, evidenced by its now passing into its third printing of the second edition, is ample reward to writer and publishers for their joint efforts on behalf of congenial home ground surroundings.

A. T. DE LA MARE CO. INC.

New York, January, 1922.

CONTENTS

(For Classified Index see pages 275 and 276)

CHAPTER I

IMPORTANCE OF CAREFUL PLANNING

Greater Enjoyment of Our Surroundings—Expression of Taste and Personality—Enjoyment of Others—Uplift to the Community—Economy of Execution—The Plan—The Grading Plan—The Planting Plan.

CHAPTER II

LOCATING THE HOUSE—EXPOSURE

CHAPTER III

ARRANGEMENT OF WALKS, DRIVES AND ENTRANCES

CHAPTER IV

CONSTRUCTION OF WALKS AND DRIVES

Cement Walks—Macadam Walks—Red Gravel Walks—Flagstone Walks—Brick Walks—Stepping Stone Walks—Terrace Walks—Dutch Tile Walks—Driveways of Cement—Waterbound Macadam—Bituminous Roads—Cement Surfacing—Cement Approaches—Gutters—Cement Gutters—Rubble Gutters—Brick Gutters—Sod Gutters—Care of Sod Gutters—Catch Basins—Gratings—Connecting Catch Basins with Drainage Lines.

CHAPTER V

LAWNS: GRADING, CONSTRUCTION AND UPKEEP

Preliminary Preparations—Lawns Ascending from Highways—Lawns Descending from Highways—Sub-Grade—Underdrainage—Lawn Grading—Larger Areas—House Below Pavement Grade—Terraces—Lawn Making—Sodding—Seeding—Grass Seeds.

CHAPTER VI

ORNAMENTAL PLANTING OF TREES AND SHRUBS

The Background for the House—Framing the House—Trees for Framing the House—Base Plantings—What to Avoid in Base Plantings—Plants for Base Plantings (Shrubs)—Plants for Base Plantings (Broad-leaved Evergreens)—Unity in Lawn Plantings—Planting for Detail—Avoid Straight Lines—Avoid Rows of Trees Along Curved Driveways—Lines of Trees for Straight Driveways—Specimen Lawn Trees—Lawn Groupings—Planting in Lawn Depressions—Planting in Valleys—Boundary Plantings—Variety in Border Plantings—Edging the Border Plantings—Evergreens in Border Plantings—Specimen Trees in Front of Border Plantings—Avoid Odd Shaped Beds in Lawn Center—Ornamental Planting on the Farm—Summary—Tree Planting—Pruning—Tree Planting with Dynamite—Moving Large Trees—Root Pruning—Care of Trees and Shrubs—Insect Pests.

CHAPTER VII

THE FLOWER GARDEN

Classification of Gardens—Garden Dimensions and Design—Garden Entrance—Garden Background—Garden Enclosures—Height of Garden Enclosures—Garden Walls—Gray Sandstone Walls—Coping—Brick Walls— The Stucco Wall—Dry Stone Walls—Hedges—Retaining Walls—Garden Steps—Piers—Walks and Beds—Width of Walks—Materials for Walks—Turf Walks—Brick Walks—Red Gravel—Stepping Stones—Flagstones—Slate— Tanbark—Borders—Garden Beds, /idth—Preparing Garden Beds—Humus— Floral Treatment—Bulbs—Annuals—Hardy Shrubs—Evergreens—Treatment of Gardens Constructed on More than One Level—Planting Around Garden Enclosures—Water in the Garden.

CHAPTER VIII

ARCHITECTURAL FEATURES OF THE GARDEN

Sundials—Bird Baths—Fountains and Pools—Depth—Construction— Pool Coping—Water Supply and Drainage—Garden Pools with Fountain Heads—Planting Near Garden Pools—Plants in the Pool—The Plants— Fish—Swimming Pools—Water Supply—Garden Seats—Garden Houses— Pergolas—Floors—Color of Wooden Garden Features.

CHAPTER IX

HARDY BORDERS AND ROSE GARDENS

Perennial Borders—Location of Hardy Borders—Avoid Borders Next to a Hedge—Turf Edge for Beds—Borders Along a Fence—Borders in the Vegetable Garden—Width of Borders—Preparation of Beds—Time to Plant—Summer Care—Arrangement of Plants in Hardy Borders—Border Beds Should not be Graduated Evenly as to Height—Background for Borders— Rose Chains in Perennial Borders—Arches Over Walks—Planting in Clumps— Bulbs and Tubers—Spring Bulbs—Summer Flowering Bulbs—Autumn Bulbs—Annuals in the Borders—Rose Gardens—Rose Garden Designs— Position—Beds—Preparation of Beds—Planting and Care—Varieties— Climbing Roses.

CHAPTER X

WILD GARDENS

The Wild Garden as an Isolated Feature—Walks—Beds—Planting in the Wild Garden—Flowers in the Wild Garden—Rock Gardens—Garden Locations—Placing of Rocks—Soil—Arrangement of Plants—Moisture Important—Garden Steps with Pockets for Plants—Time of Planting— Shrubs in Rock Gardens—Evergreens in the Rock Garden—The Heathers.

CHAPTER XI

PLANTING PLANS AND PLANTING KEYS
GLOSSARY OF TECHNICAL TERMS

ILLUSTRATIONS AND PLANS

CHAPTER I

IMPORTANCE OF CAREFUL PLANNING

How very seldom it is that the home builder gives the same thought and consideration to his outdoor home surroundings that he gives to the interior of his home ! Do we not enter a man's home the moment we set foot on the property, and not, as generally accepted, when we cross the threshold ?

There are many important reasons for the careful planning of the home grounds and I would lay particular stress on these: The greater enjoyment of our surroundings; The expression of taste and personality; The enjoyment of others; The uplift of the community; The economy of execution.

GREATER ENJOYMENT OF OUR SURROUNDINGS

To get the greatest amount of enjoyment out of our home surroundings from a purely practical standpoint the drives, the walks and other utilitarian features should be carefully planned in their relation to the house. Much thought should also be given to the location and arrangement of the garage, stable, chicken houses, and other buildings apart from the main house.

From an esthetic standpoint an even greater amount of thought should be given to the accentuating, through the correct framing of any architectural features of the house (Fig. 1); to screening out unsightly views; to the establishing of vistas; and to the locating and planting of the gardens. Every tree and shrub, every plant and plantation, should bear a definite relation, one to the other, in the general scheme.

EXPRESSION OF TASTE AND PERSONALITY

It is a very welcome thought that, as yet, the taste and refinement of the average home builder is not judged entirely by the exterior arrangement and adornment of his property. It is only when it is brought to his attention through some striking incident that the average man is brought to the realization that, to the majority of his fellows, the exterior appointments of the home stand for what he himself is. If these be cheap and tawdry he is judged to his prejudice, but if the arrangement is orderly and artistic he is credited accordingly.

It is essential. therefore, that our exterior surroundings reflect us truly. No matter how small the space, it is possible to beautify it. Among all the arts of design none is so varied in its application as that pertaining to landscape gardening. Every subject has surroundings which influence the treatment best suited to its needs; it may be the configuration of the ground, or the presence of Nature's gifts of woodland and water; it may be unattractive nearby scenes, or beautiful distant views; often, lacking all, we must create scenes within the boundaries.

The personal note continually enters into the design (Fig. 2). Some lean toward an arrangement that is stiff and formal, others to the flowing and graceful; some are partial to evergreens, others to deciduous trees and shrubs. In the floral adornment much opportunity is given for individual taste in the arrangement, the color scheme, and the seasons of bloom.

ENJOYMENT OF OTHERS

This is an unselfish reason for more careful planning and worthy of mention from that standpoint alone. Have some thought for your neighbor and the passerby. Surely such an opportunity is not to be overlooked, for of all pleasures none is to be compared with that which brings joy to the heart of others.

The owner who plans, builds and cultivates beautiful things is a benefactor, and in no channel of thought or activity is there greater or more satisfying response than in the creation of the beautiful in landscape design (Fig. 3), showing a well placed flowering specimen.

UPLIFT TO THE COMMUNITY

Nothing is so conducive to general carelessness, slovenliness and neglect as ill kept, unkempt and untidy exteriors. Likewise, nothing is more elevating and uplifting to a community than well arranged, artistic properties (Fig. 4) with well kept lawns and gardens. The effect of such surroundings is magical in its influence, and creates an insistent desire in others for the equal possession of that which is pleasing and beautiful. Figs. 5 and 6 show property before and after planting, from same point of view.

ESTABLISHING A VISTA

Fig. 1.—Well planned exteriors add greatly to the enjoyment of our surroundings. This
planting arrangement emphasizes the bay window on the stairway.—See page 9

THE PERSONAL NOTE IN THE DESIGN

Fig. 2 —Lombardy Poplars.　In the landscape treatment there is a wide choice of material
to suit the individual taste.—See pages 10 and 84

PINK FLOWERING DOGWOOD

Fig. 3.—There is a great and satisfactory response to be secured through the cultivation of beautiful trees.—See pages 10 and 84

A RESULT OF CAREFUL PLANNING

Fig. 4.—The residence here illustrated is an example of the good results to be obtained from
careful planning,—See page 10

Every house in a community should contribute toward the enjoyment of the inhabitants thereof, in some little artistic excellence, and it is inexplainable why we have so many heterogeneous, unattractive and commonplace properties in communities otherwise refined and cultured. Lack of foresight in the planning is usually the cause. It is important, therefore, that not only individuals, but communities in general plan carefully for the house surroundings.

ECONOMY OF EXECUTION

From a purely practical and financial standpoint much can be said of the importance of careful planning. Landscape work attempted without the most careful consideration of all the details is never very satisfactory and usually entails large additional expenditures for omissions and revisions. In the planning of landscape work the floral adornment is really only one of the many features which must be considered. To make the most of our opportunities, and to solve easily questions of proper grading and draining, the planning for landscape features should start with the locating of the house

From this point, questions of walk and drive arrangement, walk and drive construction, lawn grading and making, drainage, the garden and the garden details, should all be taken up in order. It is only when we have a preconceived and specific plan combining all these elements that the landscape work can proceed in an orderly and economical manner.

THE PLAN

The plan represents the conception of the designer committed to paper in a specific and comprehensive manner.

Any development, to be worth while, should be studied in the plan before attempting to execute the work on the ground.

In landscape work it is usually advisable to have two general plans—the grading plan and the planting plan.

THE GRADING PLAN

The grading plan is the essential beginning of the landscape design; the foundation on which the picture we desire to create will be realized. It shows the location and arrangement of all the practical and utilitarian features. It provides for the walks and drives

IN ITS FIRST STAGE OF LANDSCAPE DEVELOPMENT. Fig. 5.—This residence is on a lot about 200 x 200 feet. The grading is completed and some little stock has been placed in accordance with a preconceived plan.—See page 10

A STUDY IN HARMONY

Fig. 6.—Well arranged, artistic properties are an uplift to the community.   The building
is the same as that shown on page 16.—See page 10

and gives the established grades for the same. It shows in a concrete form the scheme devised for the grading and lawn making, the proper preparation of all portions on which turf is wanted. The gardens are located, grades established, enclosures and architectural features, such as fountains and pools, provided for. Questions of drainage are carefully considered and taken care of; also the water supply for lawns, gardens, fountains and pools. In fact, all the physical features are provided for and specified so that estimates for the whole or for any part of the work may easily be secured.

To prepare a grading plan there must first be a simple survey of the property. The map of the survey should show the property lines and existing features, such as large trees, buildings, roads, if any, all in their true relative dimensions and positions.

In connection with this survey levels should be taken showing the existing contours at intervals of from one to five feet, according to the slope of the ground. Also elevations at the base of trees and in the vicinity of buildings, the sidewalk elevation, and the crown of the highway.

I will not go very deeply into the technicalities of making a survey or of running levels. On small properties anyone with a knowledge of simple engineering can get all the data necessary; on larger estates a topographical survey is necessary.

THE PLANTING PLAN

The planting plan represents the horticultural and esthetic part of the design. It shows the selection and distribution of the trees and plants, each having a definite purpose and a direct bearing on the whole general scheme. In the making of such a plan all the questions that the reader will find taken up and considered in the chapters on Tree and Shrub Planting, Flower Gardens, etc., are important, and their application is shown in Chapter XI, where many concrete examples will be found.

CHAPTER II

LOCATING THE HOUSE

When planning the house, even for a small plot, much consideration should be given to the proper location. The aim should be to secure comfort, pleasure and enjoyment for the occupants, not only from the interior, but as well from as much of the exterior as may be embraced. Some thought should be given, too, to the presentment of the best architectural features of the house to the view of those from without.

EXPOSURE

The course of the sun in relation to the principal rooms of the house should be of the first importance. Fig. 7 shows the points of the compass and the comparative value of each exposure.

The location of the majority of small houses is governed by the street. The highways usually run north and south, or east and west, and so the houses are placed accordingly, invariably facing the street. This is a practice that should be discontinued if we are to get all the enjoyment possible out of our homes. There is no good reason why we should not turn the house entirely around if necessary to get the best exposure. By careful planning of the house and grounds, the kitchen wing may, if advisable, face the street with more pleasure and comfort to the occupants, and without objection to the passerby.

Figs. 8, 9, 10, 11, 12, 13 show houses variously located on small lots.

On larger estates the house should really be planned for the house site, and not the site for the house, as

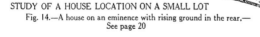

STUDY OF A HOUSE LOCATION ON A SMALL LOT

Fig. 14.—A house on an eminence with rising ground in the rear.—
See page 20

is so often the case. Here, too, we have the question of best exposure, and, in addition, consideration must be given to the background, views, and drainage.

The house should always be on an eminence, but need not necessarily be on the highest point of the ground (Fig. 14). In fact, it is often advisable to select a site with rising ground at the rear. If the rising ground be wooded the house will appear more attractive and fit more snugly into the landscape. For the best view one can always ascend to the higher point for observation and the scene will be more enjoyable for the occasional visit than it would be if it were continually within the line of vision.

It is often possible to locate the house so that the principal rooms are on the axis of some beautiful distant view. This point should not be overlooked when the site is selected.

The question of drainage is an important one. To secure comfort and health in a home the cellar and foundation should always be dry. The ideal location is one where the ground slopes directly away from the house on all four sides (Fig. 15, page 77). When such a location is not available the character of the soil should be considered and, if the ground is wet, underdrains should be provided.

The attitude usually assumed that no consideration need be given to the landscape treatment when locating houses on small plots, needs modification. While the house must be the dominant feature, a careful study of surrounding conditions, of exposure and exterior adornment, will well repay the owner.

It is much to be regretted that, on account of the generally inconsiderate placing of the house, most of our lawn area is in the rear of the house. Certainly this gives a larger measure of privacy, but too often this privacy is a detriment. People grow careless of that which is not open for all to see. Backyards provide a convenient place for the accumulation of trash and rubbish and soon the lawn is in danger of being neglected. In older communities where more consideration is given to landscape design in modeling the home grounds this condition is on the wane and the rear is considered of equal importance as the front (Figs. 11 and 12). A much better scheme is that of placing the house well to the rear of the lot, leaving but a small space at the back; or of placing the house well to one side, allowing a more extended lawn from the front to rear line. If the exposure is good the principal rooms of the house may be planned to face the lawn rather than the street.

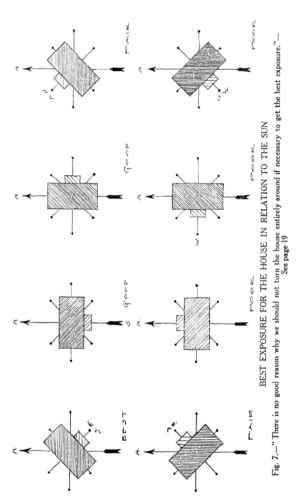

BEST EXPOSURE FOR THE HOUSE IN RELATION TO THE SUN

Fig. 7.—" There is no good reason why we should not turn the house entirely around if necessary to get the best exposure." —
See page 19

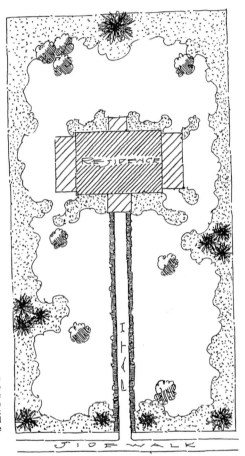

. 8.—House
ted well to
rear of the
t with
aight box
rdered
roach.—See
page 19

STUDY OF A HOUSE LOCATION ON A SMALL LOT

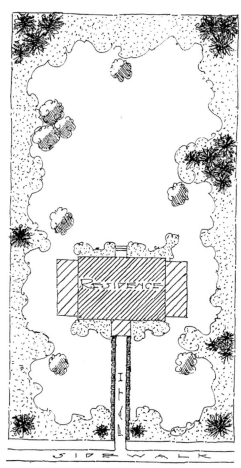

Fig. 9.—House facing the street with straight approach.—See page 19

STUDY OF A HOUSE LOCATION ON A SMALL LOT

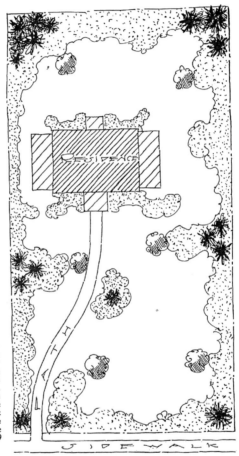

ig. 10.—
ouse located
ell to the rear
lot, showing
eatment with
urved walk,
ntering from
ie side to give
p p a r e n t
readth to the
roperty.—See
ages 19 and 29

STUDY OF A HOUSE LOCATION ON   SMALL LOT

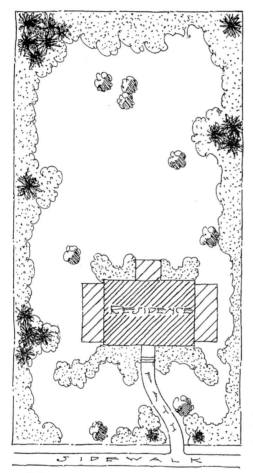

Fig. 11.—
House located
with kitchen
wing facing the
street; hidden
by the plant-
ing.—See pages
19 and 20

STUDY OF A HOUSE LOCATION ON A SMALL LOT

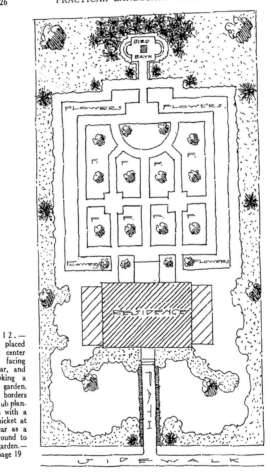

. 12.—
ie placed
he center
ot facing
rear, and
ooking a
al garden.
borders
hrub plan-
ns with a
thicket at
rear as a
ground to
garden.—
page 19

STUDY OF A HOUSE LOCATION ON A SMALL LOT

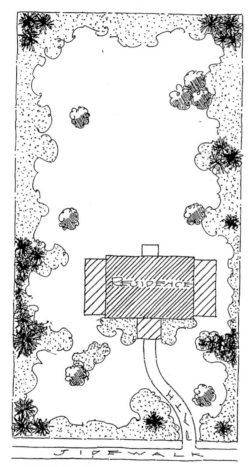

Fig. 13.-
House facin
the street, wit
curved ap
proach; lawn i
rear protecte
by the extend
ing borde
plantings.-
See page 19

STUDY OF A HOUSE LOCATION ON A SMALL LOT

Fig. 24A.—Dominant main walk with smaller service walk somewhat removed.—See page 33

CHAPTER III

ARRANGEMENTS OF WALKS, DRIVES AND ENTRANCES

After the site for the house has been located the next provision to be made concerns the best arrangement of walks and drives. Here, as in all the other features of landscape development, we have a wide latitude and are not confined to any one particular style. Every property has its individual conditions; these must be carefully considered, for they will more or less influence the designer of the drive and walk arrangement. One principle, however, is fixed: Drives and walks must be as direct as possible without being forced or twisted; they should approach by means of straight lines or by easy, graceful curves.

The house being the objective point, the trend should always be in its direction. The approach, when from the side, should be so placed that a good perspective of the house will attract the eye as one comes toward it. If some architectural feature in the house is a dominant note and worthy of attention arrange the curve so that, at a certain point, this feature will hold the center of the picture. Some such feature may be a prettily designed window, doorway, oriole bay window, or a well designed gable end.

When the house is situated at some distance from the highway, the foreground fairly level, and the property of considerable depth, a straight approach (Fig. 16) on the axis of the portal, such as the straight, box-bordered approaches of the old Southern homes, is most pleasing.

In a straight approach (Fig. 17) there should be no circles, such as we often see, around which a detour must be made before the house is reached.

On a property of little breadth the straight walk through the center bisects the lawn, leaving two tracts which are very difficult to treat. On such a property it is better to confine the walk to one side (Fig. 10) and arrange the planting to accentuate the breadth.

In the majority of cases drive and walk should enter at a right angle to the property line (Fig. 18) and finish parallel to the house. Fig. 19 shows an improper method of intersection with front pavement.

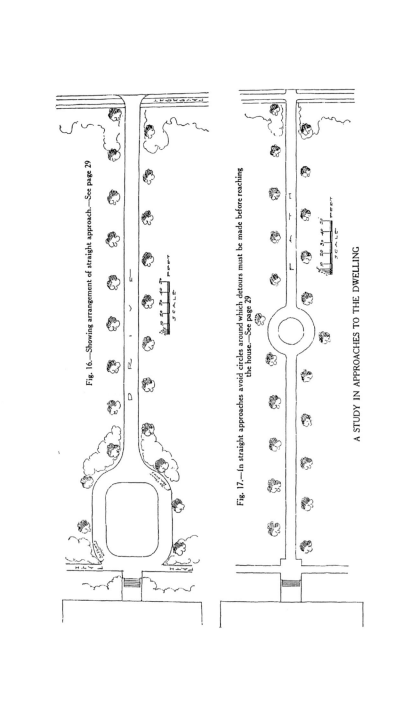

Fig. 16.—Showing arrangement of straight approach.—See page 29

Fig. 17.—In straight approaches avoid circles around which detours must be made before reaching the house.—See page 29

A STUDY IN APPROACHES TO THE DWELLING

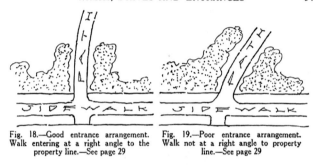

Fig. 18.—Good entrance arrangement.   Fig. 19.—Poor entrance arrangement.
Walk entering at a right angle to the   Walk not at a right angle to property
      property line.—See page 29   line.—See page 29

When a residence is located on a highway where all or nearly all of the traffic is from one point, the entrance drive (Fig. 20) should favor that direction. Such an arrangement is also desirable when the ground on the opposite side of the road is precipitous or dangerous.

The entrance gate should be toward that side of the property from which the greater portion of the traffic may be expected. It is a decided mistake to place the entrance at a point where it will necessitate the crossing of the breadth of the lot and then having

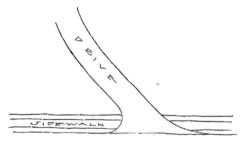

Fig. 20.—Entrance arrangement when traffic is all from one direction

to return to the house after entering the property. Where the traffic is likely to be just as great from one direction as from another it is quite practicable and pleasing to have two entrances with a semi-circular walk to the front (Fig. 21). This is feasible where the width of the lot is about equal to the distance (or a little less) from the

Fig. 21.—Walk arrangement adopted where the approach in either direction is equally important.—See page 31

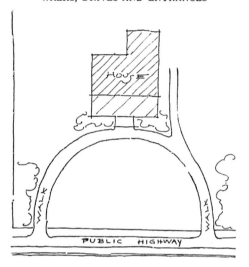

Fig. 22.—Plan showing two entrances close to party line fences

front property line to the residence. Such an arrangement is more pleasing than a straight walk down the center. It gives the appearance of the lawn expanse and apparently greater breadth.

When placing the entrance at the side (Fig. 22) a sufficient space should be left between the walk and the party line for some ornamental planting.

When it is desirable to have two entrances (Fig. 23), one may be for pedestrians and the other for vehicles.

It is well to have the service walk (Figs. 24 and 24A) somewhat removed from the front of the house if possible. The main walk leading to the front of the house should be dominant, the service walk narrower.

Where the length of the walk is sufficient it is advisable to have greater variety and beauty by having a reverse curve (Fig. 25), but this is only permissible where the distance is at least fifty feet.

Corner properties (Figs. 26 and 26A) may be entered from the corner, but such entrances are rather difficult to arrange in a satis-

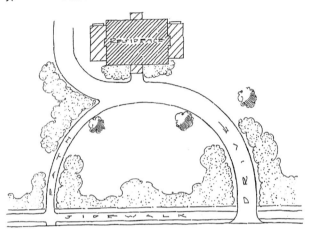

Fig. 23.—Two entrances; one for pedestrians, one for vehicles.—See page 33

factory way. Where such a scheme is adopted it is best to have the piers set well back from the line, placing them tangent to the arc of

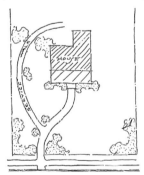

Fig. 24.—Plan showing the walk to service end of house somewhat removed from the house.—See page 33

the circle with the center at the intersection of the two property lines. This will leave two small grass plots on either side of the walk which may be pleasingly treated with ornamental plantations.

When locating a drive or walk where it is desired to avoid the direct line, it is well to select a point (Fig. 27), if practicable, where some formidable feature, such as a large tree, makes some deviation from the straight line necessary.

On properties where the residence is located not less than seventy feet from the front line, which distance is essential to give a proper turning space for cars with a large wheel-base, an entrance (Fig 28). may be placed on the axis of the house and the drive constructed to a true circle. This is a particularly appropriate arrangement for houses of classic design.

On narrow ways the entrance posts should set well back (Fig. 29) to afford an easy turn into the property. The piers defining an entrance should always be set at right angles to the roadway and where the entrance is at an angle, the fence or enclosing mater-

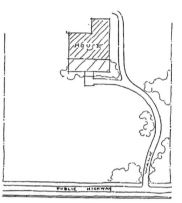

Fig 25.—Plan showing arrangement of the approach where the house sets too far back to be reached by a single arc of a circle, and a reverse is necessary.—See page 33

ial, be it hedge or wall, should extend by a graceful curve to the piers. A more pleasing and comfortable approach will be provided by keeping the fence two to four feet back from the pier, and finishing against the pier at a right angle, rather than finishing directly to the center of the face of the pier toward the highway.

The question of width and grade of approaches is of vital importance. If the elevation from the highway to the residence be great, the ascent should be as gradual as practicable, crossing the contours at the greatest possible angle. To cross a contour at a right angle gives the steepest grade and is to be avoided. When laying off the drive, set the dividers with twenty-five or fifty feet between the points and run around the contour map along a possible line of ascent, figuring out the maximum of grade desired. A six per cent. grade, that is, a rise of six feet in every one hundred feet of

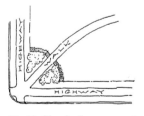

Fig. 26.—Plan showing arrangement for a corner entrance.—See page 33

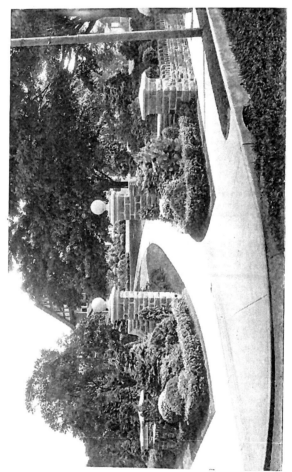

Fig. 26A.—Good arrangement of corner entrance.—See page 33

Fig. 27.—Here is an arrangement of drive adopted to save the large Maple seen in foreground. Had it not been for the tree a straight drive would have been advisable.—See page 34

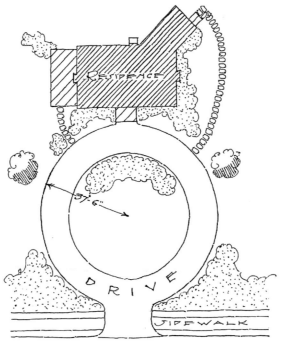

Fig. 28.—Entrance on axis of house, with drive constructed to a true circle.—See page 35

drive, is an ideal grade. A ten per cent. grade, *i.e.*, a rise of ten feet in every one hundred feet of drive, should be the maximum. A line in between these two should be established. In mountainous countries, of course, it is often necessary to establish a twelve to fifteen per cent. grade.

On adjoining properties (Fig. 30) it is possible at times to have a party drive and turn, allowing an entrance to both properties from two streets, thereby affording a maximum of convenience with economy of space.

In contracted spaces, where houses are close together (Fig. 31),

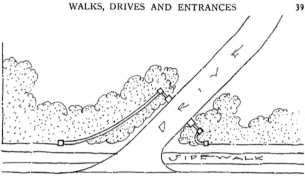

Fig. 29.—Entrance posts set back with hedge or wall finishing at a right angle to the pier.—
See page 35

party drives are preferable to having two driveways paralleling each other, and where it is only necessary to provide for motor cars, two tracks constructed of cement are to be preferred to a driveway.

Given a house on a higher level than the street, and only a short distance from pavement to house line, an arrangement of approach steps as shown in Fig. 32 will lengthen the walk, allowing it to come out to the lot line; in such a case the grass slopes on each side can still be maintained.

Where the house is located on a level higher than the street level but near the same, it will add to the interest, and picturesqueness as well, if the approach is placed at one side, as shown in Fig. 33. The terrace level here is eight feet above the pavement, and the approach is arranged in four flights of steps. The belt planting gives privacy and the approach is planned so that it does not interfere with this feature.

The drive turns (Figs. 34, 35, 36, 37 and 38), which are usually provided at the rear or side of the house, were quite roomy in former days with a diameter of fifty feet. The coming of the automobile has made it necessary to provide a diameter of seventy feet.

The elliptical or egg-shaped turn is more desirable than the true circle. This allows of a rather flat side next to the house so that a waiting vehicle will be standing in the proper position. This is not possible on a turn that is part of the arc of a circle.

When crossing a stream where a bridge is required (Fig. 39) it is advisable to cross at a right angle to the stream so that the wing walls may be built symmetrically.

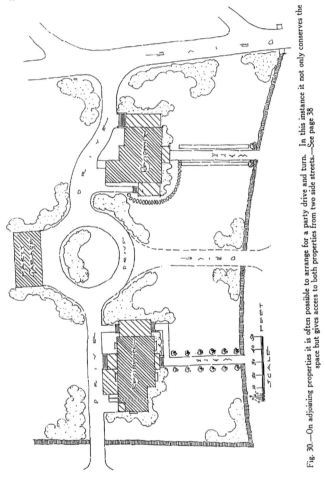

Fig. 30.—On adjoining properties it is often possible to arrange for a party drive and turn. In this instance it not only conserves the space but gives access to both properties from two side streets.—See page 38

Fig. 31.—In this view is shown a simple, practical solution of a driveway in a contracted space. This is centered on the party line and the semi-detached garages in the rear are easily accessible with ample turning space in front of them. An improvement here would have been to have two cement tracks, with grass between, rather than the entire driveway of cement. A little planting would relieve the harshness of the scene.—See pages 38, 39

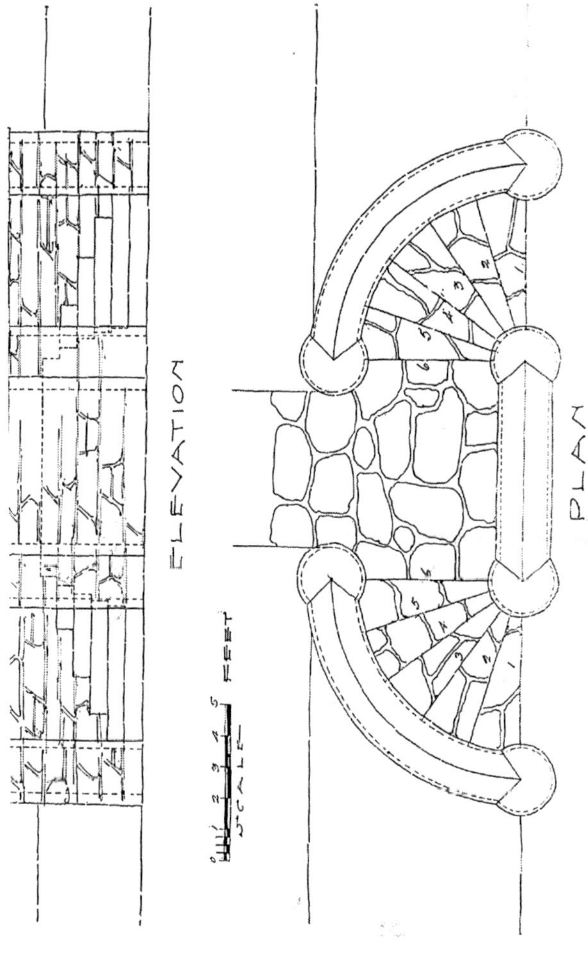

ELEVATION

SCALE   FEET

PLAN

Fig. 32.—Plan showing entrance arrangement for house situated higher than the street level but quite near the same. Such an arrangement allows the walk to extend to the lot line, thus lengthening the walk and still maintaining the slopes on either side. The figures in plan refer to the number of risers.—See page 39

Fig. 33.—Entrance arrangement for house on a level just slightly higher than the pavement.—See page 39

WIDTH OF WALKS AND DRIVES

As regards width, the walks should not be less than four feet six inches. The driveways should not be less than fourteen feet where it may be necessary to have vehicles pass, or ten feet where

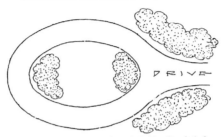

Fig. 34.—The elliptical turn is attractive and practical either directly in front of the house or at the end. The ends should be full to give ample turning space.—See page 39

the entrance is within sight of the turn. Where a great expanse of ground makes it more consistent with a proportionate entrance to have greater width, the drives may be made sixteen or eighteen feet. This greater width is really necessary now to allow motor cars to pass one another comfortably.

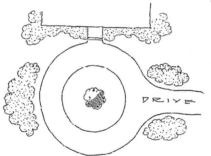

Fig. 35.—To provide turning space for the largest motor cars it is necessary to have a circle not less than seventy feet in diameter. The center should be directly on the axis of the entrance door.—See page 39

Where possible, the pedestrian walk should be combined with the drive, thus eliminating the further breaking up of the lawn. Walks and drives are necessary, but cannot be considered as pleasing landscape features where lawn space is small. Any scheme that will help to preserve the unbroken unity is to be desired.

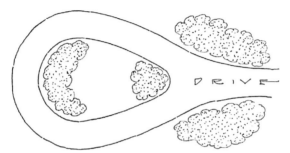

Fig. 36.—The egg-shaped turn should always be placed at the end of the house and be well concealed by plantings.—See page 39

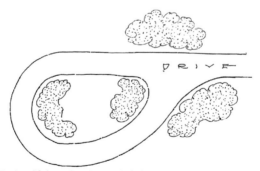

Fig. 37.—A modified pear-shaped turn with the line nearest the house parallel to it. Such a turn is less desirable for the front of the house than one of formal design.—See page 39

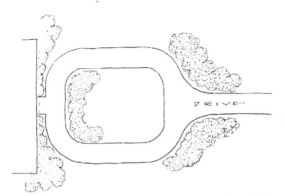

Fig. 38.—The rectangular turn is dignified and especially appropriate for Colonial houses. The center grass space may be enclosed with box edging to good effect.—See page 39

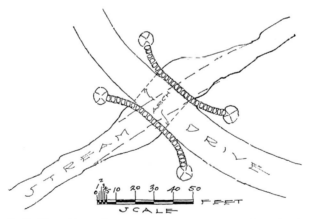

Fig. 39.—When a drive or walk crosses a stream where a bridge is required it is advisable to cross at a right angle to the stream so that the wing walls may be built symmetrically.—See page 39

CHAPTER IV

CONSTRUCTION OF WALKS AND DRIVES

Walks and driveways are features which should be built with a view to permanency. The first cost of a properly constructed walk or road should not be considered prohibitive unless equal consideration be given to the expense of maintaining a poorly constructed one.

Main walks should not be less than four feet six inches wide, and where a great expanse of ground makes it consistent with a proportionate entrance they may be five or six feet.

CEMENT WALKS

Cement makes a good, permanent material for walks (Figs. 40 and 41) and eliminates further upkeep, care and expense. It will outlast any other walk material with the exception of North River flagstone. For heavy soils a foundation of cinders eighteen inches deep is recommended. This may be reduced to six inches or omitted altogether on light and sandy soils. Three inches of concrete and one inch of cement finish make a durable walk. A three-quarter inch expansion joint should be provided every twenty to twenty-five feet. This should extend through the concrete base as well as the cement surface. The joint may be filled with asphalt or sand (Fig. 42). Cement walks have very little to recommend them from an esthetic point of view. The surface is glaring in Summer and slippery in Winter. If the top is roughened with a coarse broom when put down the surface will be more pleasing than the customary smooth finish with small and regular indentations made with a roughened roller. A cement walk with roughened surface should have a smooth margin two inches wide on each side.

The glare from cement walks may be reduced by tinting the surface coat with mortar stain. The stain should be used in small quantities, and only the very best make, care being taken when mixing to have the color thoroughly worked through the mass, otherwise it injures the quality of the cement. On an inclined walk it is advisable to have alternate lines of rough and smooth surface running at right angles to the side of the walk. The roughened strips should be three inches wide and the smooth strips two inches wide.

The use of cement has become so universal that it is really monotonous and, when possible, a material should be used that is more in tune with the natural surroundings.

MACADAM WALKS

Well kept macadam walks (Fig. 43) require more care than cement walks, but are a little more pleasing on a lawn. Use three inches of two and one-half inch stone, two inches of one and one-half inch stone, and one inch of breaker dust. Wet thoroughly and roll to a hard and even surface. Quarry spawls may be used for the two and one-half inch stone if securable near at hand; this would materially reduce the cost. Such walks cost about seventy cents per square yard under favorable conditions. A macadam walk is more satisfactory from a landscape point of view than cement. On properties where steep grades are encountered provision must be made for proper drainage, else the cost of maintenance will be prohibitive. Gutters and catch basins should be installed at intervals. Macadam walks should have a crown of one-half inch to the foot.

RED GRAVEL WALKS

A surface of one to two inches of red gravel on the same base as recommended for the macadam path makes a walk that is really the best for paths within the property borders. Gravel walks are subject to surface washing and should be provided with gutters and catch basins.

FLAGSTONE WALKS

Flagstone walks, made with flags of North River blue stone or Indiana limestone, are the most serviceable of all walks.

The flags should be two to three inches thick and should be laid on a sub-base of cinders not less than six inches deep. Wet the cinders and tamp them to a hard, even surface; over this place one inch of bar sand compacted as a cushion for the flags. After the slabs are leveled and firmed the joints should be pointed with a flat cement mortar joint.

It is customary to lay flags cut in single blocks of various lengths to the *full* width of the walk.

Fig. 40.—Cross section through cement walk.—See page 47

In recent years the custom, copied from abroad, has been introduced of breaking up the flags and laying them with random joints (Figs. 44 and 45), giving a very picturesque effect. The interstices between the stones may be pointed with cement mortar one to one and one-half inches wide, or the joints may be made from two to three inches wide, without mortar, allowing the grass to come up

Fig. 41.—Cross section through cement walk, with cement curb.—See page 47

in the spaces. The latter is much more attractive when it is possible to keep the turf green by copious waterings during droughts.

Slate (Fig. 46) is sometimes used in a similar manner, and, coming as it does in various shades, some beautifully marked with rich brown splashes, makes a very pleasing appearance. When the slabs of slate are broken to be laid with random joints, with grass

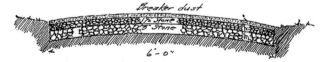

Fig. 43.—Cross section through macadam walk.—See page 48

Fig. 42.—" Cement walks are serviceable, but have little to recommend them from an esthetic standpoint. The surface is glaring in Summer and slippery in Winter." —See page 47

in the interstices, they may be laid directly on the turf where they will eventually settle into place with all the appearance of having "just happened there."

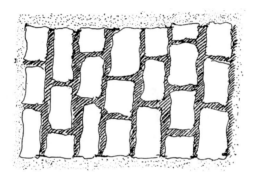

Fig. 44.—Walk of broken flagstones laid with wide mortar joints.—See page 49

BRICK WALKS

The brick walk, properly laid, is pleasing to the eye and makes a good contrast with the turf. It does not lend itself well to curved lines and so should be used only where straight lines predominate.

Bricks may be laid on either a cinder or a concrete base. A cinder base should consist of six inches of clean cinders with one

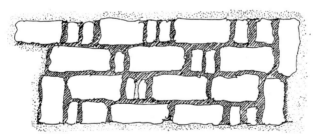

Fig. 45.—Walk of broken flagstones laid with wide mortar joint.—See page 49

A SLATE WALK

Fig. 46.—Slate makes a pleasing walk, coming as it does in various shades, some slates being
beautifully marked with rich brown splashes.—See page 49

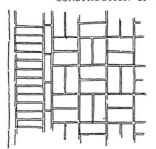

Fig. 47.—If a brick walk is six feet wide or more a border such as shown here makes an attractive finish.—See page 51

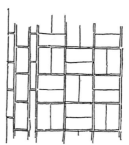

Fig. 48.—A good treatment for brick walks less than six feet wide.—See page 51

inch of bar sand as a cushion. The concrete base, which is more expensive, should consist of five inches of concrete with a one inch sand cushion. A concrete base preserves a true alignment and prevents upheavals. A brick walk should always have a curb of bricks laid on edge or end.

Figs. 47, 48, 49, 50 and 51 show various designs for brick walks.

The old diagonal fashion (Fig. 52) gives an atmosphere of Colonial times and will probably continue to be looked upon with favor by those who contemplate the construction of garden walks. This design in particular does not lend itself well to curved lines, so its use is limited to positions where straight lines predominate.

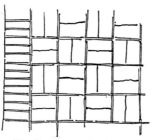

Fig. 49.—An attractive border of brick laid on edge the full width.—See page 51

Fig. 50.—Basket pattern. Half bricks on edge for a border.—See page 51

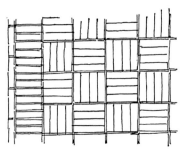

Fig. 51.—The basket pattern of bricks on edge is not so pleasing, as it shows too many mortar lines.—See page 53

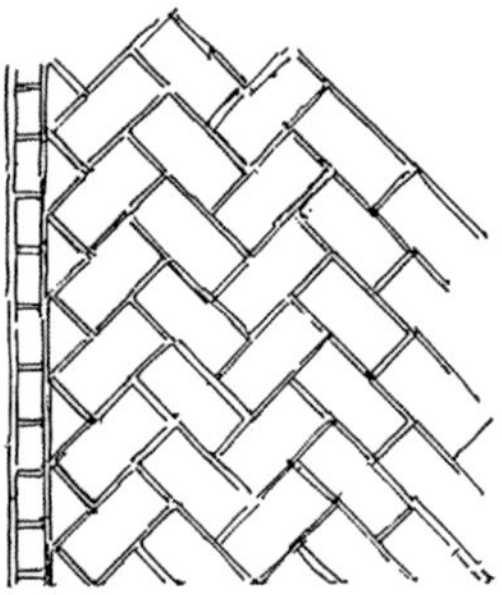

Fig. 52.—The old-fashioned diagonal or herringbone pattern in bricks or tile. Good where straight lines predominate.—See pages 51 and 53

When the bricks are laid in place the joints should be filled with bar sand or grouted and pointed with cement mortar. The mortar joints are expensive but more lasting than the sand and prevent weeds or grass from growing in the interstices.

The texture of brick walks may be greatly improved by applying an occasional coating of boiled linseed oil.

STEPPING STONE WALKS

Stepping stones of local field stone (Figs. 53 and 54) are very naturalistic and picturesque. They may be laid in a single or double line; the double line for walks of importance, the single line for secondary paths. The stones should be set into the sod to a depth that will bring the flat surface level with the turf to allow of the lawn mower passing over. Space the stones twenty inches apart, center to center, using stones not less than twelve inches wide nor larger than eighteen inches wide. Vary the stones and avoid placing pieces of the same dimensions close together.

TERRACE WALKS

Terrace walks (Fig. 55) should be of rather generous dimensions, never less than five feet wide, while on very broad terraces the walk may be from seven to ten feet wide. It is good practice on broad terraces to place the walk nearer the house than the edge of the

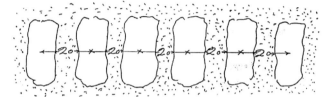

Fig. 53.—Stepping stone walk; the stones, gathered from local sources, are laid twenty inches apart, center to center.—See page 54

terrace, that is, to have more turf area on the outside of the walk than between the walk and the building.

Any of the materials mentioned for walk construction are suitable for terrace walks. Something substantial looking, such as the flags, or bricks, are most appropriate, and should always be laid on a firm base.

DUTCH TILE

Dutch tile, sometimes called brick tile on account of the similarity in texture, should be more generally used for terrace walks. These should always be laid on a concrete base with mortar joints not less than one-half inch wide.

All paving material should be laid true and even, and on walks

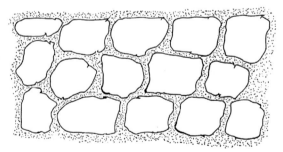

Fig. 54.—Field stones laid in turf are very pleasing where a walk of some width is desired.—See page 54

TREATMENT OF THE TERRACE WALK

Fig. 55.—Terrace walks should be of generous dimensions, never less than five feet wide.—
See page 54

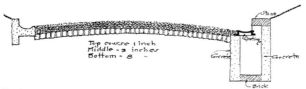

Top course 1 inch
Middle " 3 inches
Bottom " 8 "

Fig. 56.—A cross section through a waterbound macadam road with cement curb and
gutter.—See page 62

it is essential to give them a crown of one-half of an inch to the
foot. Terrace walks should follow the general slope of the ground.

DRIVEWAYS OF CEMENT

On small properties the cement driveway is advisable and superior
to any other. Oftentimes two cement tracks, with sod between, will
take care of all traffic and yet apparently reduce the space taken up
by the drive.

WATERBOUND MACADAM

Most of the driveways built today are those which are known as
Telford roads (Fig. 56). These are usually constructed of twelve
inches of stone over all. An eight-inch foundation is provided of
hard quarry stone, laid on edge, with the longest dimension placed

Fig. 57.—Very often the large stone for the base course in the drive may be quarried on the
property.—See page 58

AN IDEAL BITUMINOUS ROAD

Fig. 58.—A " Tarvia " macadam road. Free from dust and of good wearing qualities.—
See page 59

at a right angle to the side line of the drive. Very often this large
stone can be found on the property (Fig. 57). After the stones are
placed they should be gone over with napping hammers and made
fairly even by breaking off the irregular edges; the pieces of stone
so broken off should be used to fill in chinks. Over this should be
placed three inches of one and one-half inch stone. Then a light
covering of three-quarter inch stone may be placed as a binder and
finished with clean breaker dust. The drive should be rolled before and after placing the three-quarter inch stone, with a roller
weighing not less than five tons. The three-quarter inch stone
and the dust should never be mixed together; the dust will work
through and the stone find the surface, making it rough and troublesome. When rolling the finished surface it should be wetted constantly until a wave of water appears in front of the roller.

BITUMINOUS ROADS

The automobile is a new factor to be figured with in the construction of drives, as we find the waterbound roads are not very

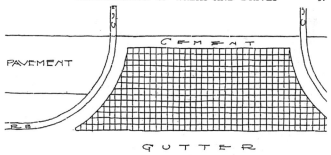

CONSTRUCTION OF A CEMENT APPROACH
Fig. 59.—Showing the construction of a cement driveway approach

satisfactory when subjected to the wear and tear of motor travel. Dust prevention must also be considered.

To strengthen the wearing surface of the macadam and reduce the amount of dust, some kind of refined tar is best (Fig. 58). There are many such preparations on the market today and each carries with it proper specifications for applying. This should preferably be applied during hot weather, the penetration then being more thorough.

CEMENT SURFACING

In some localities it is impossible to secure a stone with any adhesive qualities. Where such a condition exists run a cement grout, consisting of one part Portland cement to three parts of sharp sand, over the surface. Over this place a thin layer of the breaker dust and go over with a splint broom, thus roughening up the surface to prevent skidding. This makes a good, practical driveway that will stand a lot of traffic without unraveling or costing anything for maintenance. The bituolithic binders may be used for the same purpose provided the stone is of cubical form.

CEMENT APPROACHES

At the point where the drive intersects the highway it is advisable to pave the surface from the outside edge of the gutter to the property line (Fig. 59). It is necessary, usually, to increase the drive incline at this point to meet the gutter grade, and if macadam is used there is constant erosion. The paved surface prevents this and affords a hard surface for pedestrians. Such an approach should

GUTTER CONSTRUCTION

Fig. 60.—A pleasing and serviceable drive defined by a gutter constructed of Belgian blocks.—See page 61

be constructed of cement or brick. If cement is used the surface should be roughened to prevent slipping.

Where the walk or drive grade is not steep gutters will not be required and a few catch basins will take care of the surface water (Fig. 60). If the surface over which the water gathers is great enough the road will be more pleasing and serviceable when defined by a curb or gutter.

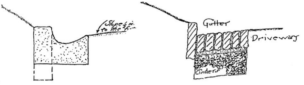

·Fig. 61.—Section of a concrete gutter and curb.—See page 59   Fig. 62.—A section showing the construction of a rubblestone gutter and curb

CEMENT GUTTERS

Where gutters (Fig. 61) are required the most satisfactory, although undoubtedly artificial in appearance, is the cement curb and gutter combined. This forms a good, substantial feature against which to finish the sod on one side and the road metal on the other. The foundation on heavy soils should be extended to a depth of eighteen inches.

Use clean boilerhouse cinders or stone spawls as a foundation to within five inches of the finished grade; on this place the concrete, consisting of a mixture of one part Portland cement to four parts of sand and five parts of crushed stone. The finish coat should consist of one part Portland cement and two parts of sharp sand, troweled even and hard.

RUBBLE GUTTERS

The rubble curb and gutter (Fig. 62), built of quarried or field stone laid on edge and swept with chips, is very suitable for suburban and country districts. Such gutters should be not less than eighteen inches wide.

An objectionable feature of the rubble gutter is that the grass and weeds grow up through the interstices. Where the stone is laid on a good foundation of clean cinders, twelve or eighteen inches deep, the joints may be grouted with Portland cement mortar, using three parts sand and one part cement. This grouting will prevent the grass and weed growth.

BRICK AND SOD GUTTERS

Brick gutters should be laid on a four-inch concrete base and firmed with bar sand or a cement grouting. A concave brick gutter, eighteen inches wide, should slope three inches to the center. If a curb is desired the brick should be laid on end with the gutter finishing against it, and sloping two to three inches to the curb.

The most pleasing gutters are those of turf. Such gutters should be concave, with a slope toward the center of from one to two inches to the foot. A gutter four feet wide should slope two inches to the center. A gutter six feet wide should slope one inch to the foot, giving a three inch depression as the minimum. The carrying capacity is increased by the increased breadth. Where the area to be drained is large the gutter may have a maximum dip of six inches. After sodding the gutter a light coating of soil should be spread over the surface and sown with a good quality of grass seed.

In sod gutters inlets are necessary to carry off the surface water. The number required will be governed by the area to be drained. In rolling ground with large areas it is usually necessary to place them every fifty feet. When building a driveway where sod gutters have been adopted the drive surface should be finished even with the soil so that the water will run off into the gutters.

Turf gutters should be formed of tough sod cut from an old pasture. Before laying the sod, the concave surface should be covered with three or four inches of good soil and made true and even with a template. This can easily be pulled along as the soil is deposited and a uniform surface made for the reception of the sod.

CARE OF SOD GUTTERS

Every Spring the edge of the gutter should be tamped down along the edge of the drive, as the frost will heave it higher than the road metal. It should be rolled when the lawn is gone over in early Spring after the frost is out of the ground.

CATCH BASINS

Catch basins (Fig. 56) may be constructed of concrete or brick, whichever material is more convenient to the operation. The concrete construction is simple and should consist of a mixture of one part Portland cement, three parts of sand, and four parts of crushed stone. Side walls should be six inches thick plumb, and an opening left for the outlet pipe one foot above the bottom of the basin. This will allow a space for the sand and debris to collect.

The side walls for brick catch basins should be at least nine inches thick, built of straight, hard, building bricks that will ring clear when hit together. They should be laid in a Portland cement mortar consisting of one part cement to two parts of sharp sand.

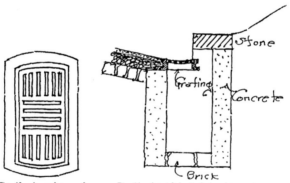

Fig. 63.—A good type of
catch basin grating

Fig. 64.—A catch basin designed to receive a
large volume of water

GRATINGS

Catch basins should be provided with gratings (Fig. 63) with ample open spaces between the bars for a free intake of all water. Small openings become clogged with leaves and are useless.

Where a large volume of water is to be taken care of it is well to build the basin back six or eight inches beyond the iron grating and place a coping stone over it, with an opening three inches wide, for the full length of the grating (Fig. 64).

CONNECTING CATCH BASINS WITH DRAINAGE LINES

Where road drainage is connected to the sewage disposal system it is necessary to have a running trap between the sewerage line and each connection with the catch basins. In this event care should be exercised to see that all pieces of pipe are free from flaws and the joints packed with oakum before cementing the sections together.

Fig. 69.—Where the ground is slightly undulating, the aspect is most pleasing if the surface is unbroken to the base of the house, with only sufficient slope to drain off the surface water. The view illustrates the charm of a lawn treated in this manner

CHAPTER V

***

LAWNS—GRADING, CONSTRUCTION AND UPKEEP

No single feature connected with the landscape development of a property is so important as the lawn. We speak here of a lawn principally in the sense of an open grass plot, not in the composite sense of turf and plantings that we often think of when the term "lawn" is used. Possibly the old English term "greensward" would be a better word to use to describe a lawn in its single meaning, and we may revert to its use occasionally to keep the thought fixed.

The lawn is the base that we must work on to make a pleasing landscape picture. It is the central feature and requires strict attention to all details. It is the element in landscape gardening that continually lends or takes. It is framed by pleasing shrubbery borders and, in turn, frames lovely vistas. Made perfectly level, and hedged in tightly with border plantings, the whole property looks cramped and contracted. Given gentle slopes and slight depressions, and allowed to run off here and there, a feeling of expanse is created. A house set lower than the street level may, by care in the lawn grading, be made to appear much higher than it is. In these and in many other ways does the lawn enter largely into the best landscape development.

PRELIMINARY PREPARATIONS

Good greenswards are not often met with, and the majority of failures may be traced to lack of forethought in the making, that is, lack of forethought in the physical construction. Too often soil and seed alone enter into the question and no thought of drainage or future upkeep. Such lawns are never a success and can never be improved unless torn up and a fresh start made.

Let us look well, then, to a right beginning, so that our finished lawn will be a unison of the proper relation to house, best drainage and construction, proper seeding, and ease of upkeep. In order to do this it is essential that we familiarize ourselves thoroughly with all existing physical conditions before the work is started.

A LAWN ASCENDING FROM A HIGHWAY

Fig. 65.—Cross section showing proper grading of portion around a residence located on ground ascending from the highway.—See page 67

Before the excavation of the cellar is made all the top soil, which extends to a depth of from four to twelve inches, should be removed and stacked in convenient piles for future use. It is well, too, to remove the surface soil for a distance of fifteen to twenty-five feet beyond the lines of all the buildings, as the construction work is apt to destroy all the soil close by.

This important feature is often overlooked, for, as a general rule, the landscape gardener is not called in for advice until the residence and other buildings have been completed.

Very frequently, too, houses are not properly situated as regards the elevation of the floor level above the surrounding grades of the ground. It has been the author's experience that a large percentage of the residences have been set entirely too low. It is very much better to err in the opposite direction, as height may be overcome by a proper planting at the base of the house in case there is not a sufficient amount of soil available to make the necessary fill.

A LAWN DESCENDING FROM A HIGHWAY

Fig. 66.—Cross section showing proper grading around a residence located on ground descending from the highway.—See page 67

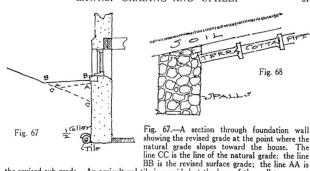

Fig. 67

½ Cellar

Tile

Fig. 68

Fig. 67.—A section through foundation wall showing the revised grade at the point where the natural grade slopes toward the house. The line CC is the line of the natural grade; the line BB is the revised surface grade; the line AA is the revised sub-grade. An agricultural tile is provided at the base of the well to prevent seepage running into the cellar.

Fig. 68.—A section showing the construction of a dry well for surface water.—See page 68

LAWNS ASCENDING FROM HIGHWAYS

If the house is located on ground ascending from the highway, with still higher ground in the rear of the house site, it is necessary to provide a plateau for the building (Fig. 65).   This should be approached with a bold hand and the cutting out behind the building made broad and generous to avoid a sense of being shut in.   The revised surface should be sloped away from the building in all directions.   The minimum fall on the axis of the building should be one-eighth of an inch to the foot, while from the center toward the ends of the building at least one-quarter of an inch to the foot should be provided for.

LAWNS DESCENDING FROM HIGHWAYS

Somewhat the same conditions prevail on ground descending from the highway (Fig. 66).   In both instances the precaution of waterproofing the house foundations, either with a tar paint or by building them of waterproofed concrete, should not be overlooked.

SUB-GRADE

The lawn surface around the house should have a minimum slope of one-half an inch to the foot and care should be taken to see that the sub-grade has a similar inclination (Fig. 67).   No matter how great the surface slope away from the house is, if the old natural grade pitches toward the foundation walls the water percolates through the new fill and runs down the foundation walls to the cellar. Such a condition may also be overcome by filling in around the house with a stiff clay, if available, this to be thoroughly tamped or, still better, puddled. This sub-grade should have a slope of at least two inches to the foot for a distance of four feet from the foundation walls. Beyond that it may be reduced to one-half inch to the foot.

UNDERDRAINAGE

Occasionally the ground falls away enough to have a point lower than the cellar floor. In such instances it is a wise precaution against a damp cellar to introduce a three or four inch agricultural tile around the base, laid with open joints and half collars placed over each joint to prevent the soil from falling in and clogging the orifice. Where drive and walk drains exist this line of pipe may be connected with that system.

LAWN GRADING

Generally speaking, the surface beyond the buildings may be left as found so far as the contour of the ground is concerned; the exception being small properties where it is possible to modify all lines of grade to suit the house without entailing too great an expense.

LARGER AREAS

On larger properties it is only necessary to soften steep depressions or humps by lengthening the slopes, provided, of course, that the surface water may be drained off. Where depressions are large and the work entailed to carry the surface water off over the surface is too extensive, a catch basin should be provided. From this the drain may be projected to a lower point of grade or to a small well. Such a well should be about three feet in diameter and four feet deep (Fig. 68), this to be filled with stone to within twelve inches of the top, over which place the top soil. Draining to such a well is preferable to running it out on the surface. Drainage to a well spreads by seepage over a large area. In case a sewer line has been installed in the streets it is much better to connect with it, but extreme care should be taken to see that the line of pipe is properly trapped to prevent sewer gas from backing up in the pipe lines.

CORRECT GRADING FOR HOUSE BELOW PAVEMENT GRADE

Fig. 70.—A section showing revised grade for lawn when the house is located lower than the pavement

HOUSE BELOW PAVEMENT GRADE

Quite frequently topographical conditions are encountered that make it necessary to set the house below the grade of the pavement. (Fig. 70.) In such cases the site selected should be just as far back from the property line as practicable, the slope from the

CORRECT GRADING WHEN HOUSE IS ON STREET LEVEL

Fig. 71.—A section showing concave lawn surface where the pavement and house grades are on the same level. The convex surface as shown by the dotted line is not so good, as it apparently shortens the distance.—See page 70

house to a point one-fifth to one-third the total distance from the house to the property line to be made rather sharp, with the longer slope from the property line to the established low point. This treatment will seemingly lift the house up and is more pleasing than a grade with the longer slope falling from the house.

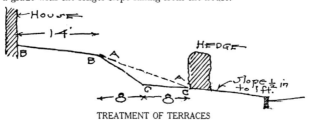

TREATMENT OF TERRACES

Fig. 72.—When the distance CC is less than BB it is better to eliminate the slope BC and grade along the lines of AA.—See page 70

Should the point of grade at the house and at the pavement
be on the same level (Fig. 71), and provided the house is located
well back from the property line, the appearance will be greatly
enhanced by making a depression between the house and the street.
To do this the elevation of the ground at one side must be below the
lowest point of depression. It is very apparent that a lawn graded
to such a profile would give a sense of distance while, on the other
hand, a convex line would tend to shorten the distance.

TERRACES

When to introduce terraces is a problem that requires careful
consideration. On a ground slightly undulating and where the
surface slopes are rather gentle, the effect is more pleasing if the
lawn rolls right up to the walls of the house. On more rugged
ground, where there is a great variation in levels between the various
corners of the house, a level plateau surrounding the house is better.

The width of the terrace will depend somewhat on the size of
the building and the lot; ordinarily it should not be less than
fourteen feet; if there is to be a paved terrace or a porch, the
turf terrace, being of different texture, should be at least one-third
greater in width. It is very unsatisfactory to have a terrace of
greater breadth than the remaining area between the bottom of
the slope and the line of the property.

When a condition exists wherein the space is not great enough to
treat it as above recommended it is more advisable to have the
slope extend from the plateau at the house to the property line by
a gentle inclination (Fig. 72). The surface should slope at least
one-half inch to the foot, and the slope from the terrace to the surrounding lawn grade should not be steeper than one foot to two feet,
while one to three is much preferable as the grass is more easily cut
on such a slope than on one with a sharper inclination (Fig. 73).
The slope should always be uniform and the line next to the house
should be parallel to the building, while the bottom line of the terrace may vary according to the slope of the abutting lawn. When
close to the house, where straight lines predominate, it is best to
have two lines of the terrace well defined.

A terrace along a property line (Fig. 74) may be graded to a
convex surface at the top, and at the bottom it may be given a concave surface, thus gracefully merging the steeper grades into the
more gentle ones at top and bottom.

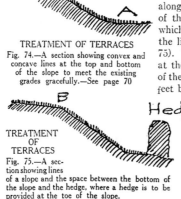

TREATMENT OF TERRACES

Fig. 74.—A section showing convex and concave lines at the top and bottom of the slope to meet the existing grades gracefully.—See page 70

TREATMENT
OF
TERRACES

Fig. 75.—A section showing lines of a slope and the space between the bottom of the slope and the hedge, where a hedge is to be provided at the toe of the slope.

Where hedges are to be planted along property lines, at the top of the terrace, or at the bottom, which is the better place for them, the lines should be decided (Fig. 75). When a hedge is to be planted at the bottom of a slope, the toe of the slope should be at least three feet back from the line. This will provide a level space to stand on and trim the hedge with much more comfort than standing on a slope. The plants, too, will thrive better. Slopes should always be sodded where a good, clean turf is procurable.

LAWN MAKING

While the building is in course of construction the soil will become very much compacted by the teams and mechanics, a condition which is rather bad for the sustaining of grass. All the areas which have been trodden down hard should be loosened up before the surface soil is replaced. Better turf can usually be grown on soil that is broken up to some depth.

When the grading is being done it is well to take account of the nature of the soil and ascertain what treatment may be necessary for the production of a satisfactory stand of grass. If the soil is of a sandy or gravelly nature, or if it is lacking in humus, barnyard manure should be spread and thoroughly assimilated with the top soil. Should the soil be of a stiff, clayey nature, equal parts of sand and manure should be mixed through the top soil. This will make the soil more porous and the rain and air will reach the roots of the grass.

Another point to look to, at this time, is the digging and preparation of holes for any trees or specimen shrubs that it is planned to locate on the lawn. Such work can be done to much better advantage now than if left until after the rolling and seeding.

Sometimes it is necessary to raise the grade on ground where large trees are established. A fill of a foot or more of soil over the roots of most trees will kill them very quickly. Such trees may be preserved by building a dry retaining wall with a diameter at least two feet greater than the trunk. If the lawn is of sufficient size and the trees form a clump, a depression may be left around them.

Now that the rough work is out of the way, drainage attended to, grades established and terraces built, the question of the real making of the new lawn confronts us.

The changed conditions make it necessary to provide new soil close to the house and on properties of small dimensions it may be necessary to resurface the entire area. Wherever fill is needed just as good soil as can be procured should be used and at least four inches of good top soil provided for the surface.

If the old turf needs remaking it should be dug or plowed to the depth of a spade, the soil being turned well over, stones and weed roots removed and large clods broken up.

Manuring or fertilizing is an important question. Experts claim that one ton of grass removes from the soil thirty-four pounds of nitrogen, thirty-six pounds of potash and seventeen pounds of phosphoric acid. It is largely these substances, therefore, that must be provided. Stable manure, if obtainable, is very satisfactory. Apply at the rate of one load per one hundred square yards and dig or fork it into the soil. Care should be exercised to see that the manure is not buried too deeply, else it will not be within reach of the new young grass—four inches is a good average depth. A good commercial fertilizer, containing four per cent. nitrogen, eight per cent. phosphoric acid and ten per cent. potash, will be found to give very satisfactory results. This should be applied at the rate of ten pounds per one hundred square yards and raked in. Fertilizers that are highly soluble should not be used on sandy soils, as they will quickly dissolve after rainfalls, be washed beyond the reach of the roots and so wasted. This same remark covers all commercial fertilizers applied in a wet season or a time of drought. In one case they are washed away, and in the other they lie about the surface and waste.

After manuring, the ground should be prepared to receive the seed. The soil should be carefully gone over with an iron toothed rake, all large stones removed, clods broken up and weed roots taken out, then rolled and raked until the surface becomes firm and fine; it should be so firm that walking over it leaves no footprints.

TREATMENT OF TERRACES

Fig. 73.—This house is located on ground where the slope was so great that it was necessary to have a high terrace at one end, and run out to meet the natural grade at the other. It is always best to have a terrace as wide as practicable under such conditions, so that the end of the residence at the low point of the slope will have a more substantial setting.—See page 70

SODDING

The spaces along the walks and drives should be sodded to maintain the edge. It is well, too, to sod the space directly against the house, to prevent any soiling of the wall surfaces by splashing.

SEEDING

Time of sowing and the best seed are subjects of equal importance. Unless we look well to these two essentials we may have our trouble in the manuring and preparation of the ground set to naught. Spring and Fall are the best seasons for sowing, preferably the months of April and September. Lawns seeded late in the Fall should be given a mulch as a Winter protection.

GRASS SEEDS

The varieties of grasses suitable for the making of a good lawn are limited. The general desire is for a close turf of pleasing color. Soil and climatic conditions will enter largely into the right selection. (The recommendations which follow apply to the Atlantic coast region north of Washington, D. C., and the Allegheny region as far south as northern Georgia.)

Kentucky Blue Grass is the best all-around lawn grass and will thrive in any good lawn, providing it receives a generous but not excessive amount of moisture.

In soils of very light character Red Top, Rhode Island Bent, Creeping Bent or White Clover are good.

On account of the varied conditions met with, a mixture including the above named kinds in varying proportion, is usually most satisfactory.

Seed of the highest grade from a reliable house should be purchased and sown at the rate of five bushels (100 lbs.) to the acre; or, one quart to 300 sq. ft. This will allow for a very generous seeding, which is much to be preferred to seed sparsely scattered.

Grass seeds will vary in weight as to the number of pounds to the bushel. In recleaned seeds of a high grade, Blue Grass should run from twelve to fifteen pounds to the bushel; Red Top extra recleaned, thirty pounds to the bushel; Creeping Bent, twenty pounds; Rhode Island Bent, fourteen pounds; White Clover, sixty pounds. A good grass seed mixture should average twenty pounds to the bushel.

A calm day should be chosen for the seeding, otherwise it is

LAWNS GRADED AROUND TREES

Fig. 76.—Sometimes it is necessary to raise the grade on ground where large trees are established.   A fill of a foot or more of soil over the roots of a tree will kill it very quickly.   Such trees may be preserved by building a dry retaining wall, with a diameter at least two feet greater than the trunk.—See page 72

hard to get an equal distribution. The seeding should be done in two directions, dividing the seed into two lots, one lot being sown at a right angle to the other. After sowing, the seed should be covered to a depth of about one-quarter of an inch; this may be done by raking the surface lightly. The ground should then be rolled with a light roller. When the young grass is about one and one-half inches high it should be rolled again and the first cutting made when about two inches high. The machine should be set quite high for the first cutting. All bare and thin places should be promptly reseeded.

The lawn having been thoroughly established it is very essential that careful and systematic attention be given to the upkeep; otherwise it will deteriorate very quickly.

Weeds are always a menace and, linked with Fall Grass, should be continually fought against. Newly made lawns often contain many weeds of an annual nature which disappear after a few cuttings. The perennial weeds are persistent and can only be effectively removed by hand. The dandelion and plantain are exceedingly troublesome and must be removed, root and top. This may be done with a sharp chisel or a three-pronged fork. Weeding forks for this purpose are to be had at all seed stores. Boys can usually be had to do this work at the rate of a few cents per hundred.

During moist weather, when the grass is making vigorous growth, it should be cut about once in a week and an occasional rolling will help greatly to keep the surface firm. Grass does poorly on a loose surface. In hot, dry weather the blades in the machine should be raised so that the grass will be left of sufficient length to afford some protection to the roots. Too close cutting during Midsummer weakens the turf and makes it more susceptible to the inroads of Fall grass.

Every Spring a fertilizer should be applied that will supply per acre one hundred pounds of potash and fifty pounds of available phosphoric acid. Apply at the same time a top dressing of three hundred pounds of nitrate of soda. The nitrate should be applied again at the end of June, using one hundred pounds to the acre. Such fertilizers are to be preferred to stable manures, as they are less offensive, require less labor to apply, and are free of weed seeds.

It is possible sometimes to renovate a wornout lawn without

entirely remaking, by top dressing with a compost consisting of equal parts of soil and manure, to which about ten per cent. of tankage has been added. Such a top dressing is recommended also for lawns made on shallow soils.

In the Southern States it is quite impossible to establish a permanent greensward that will look well at all seasons. The only grass that will succeed with any degree of satisfaction is the Bermuda Grass (*Capriola dactylon*). This grass dies to the ground in the Winter, but is good during the Spring, Summer and early Autumn. Lawns of this grass are made by cutting up the roots of old plants and setting the small tufts of root about twelve inches apart, mulching with well rotted manure. For Winter effect on terraces or lawn close to the house English perennial Rye may be sown.

STUDY OF A HOUSE LOCATION ON A SMALL LOT

Fig. 15.—" The ideal location is one where the ground slopes away from the house on all four sides."—See page 20

FRAMING THE HOUSE

Fig. 77.—'', In addition to a suitable background, it is essential that the residence be properly framed by plantations at both ends.'' It is not always advisable to plant the trees directly at the ends of the building.   Usually a point forward of the front line gives a better effect.   The base plantings of broad-leaved evergreens are effective at all times of the year.—See pages 80 and 85

CHAPTER VI

———

ORNAMENTAL PLANTING OF TREES AND SHRUBS

Although the drives, walks and topography contribute much toward the general effect of the home grounds, it is upon the embellishment of the whole, through the proper selection and arrangement of the ornamental plantings, that we depend for the picturesque beauty and grace of the lawn.

THE BACKGROUND FOR THE HOUSE

A first consideration is a good background for the house and, where one does not already exist, plantations of trees should be located that will give this effect as quickly as possible. In such plantings it is advisable to set more trees than will be needed eventually, the principle being that trees planted close together encourage a greater top growth and thus attain height more quickly than trees given ample space for development; in the latter instance much of the strength going toward lateral growth.

The Tulip Poplar (*Liriodendron tulipifera*) is a rapid growing tree with all the needed qualities for a background planting. Under favorable conditions the Tulip Poplar will reach a height of one hundred or more feet. The foliage, rich and glossy, the attractively lobed leaves, the large, tulip-like green and yellow flowers, and a straight, towering main stem are all attributes of this grand tree. If this tree is used it should be set well back from the house line, as the branches spread to such an extent and rise to such a height that they will form a most pleasing canopy over any smaller and slower growing trees which may be planted between it and the residence.

Other good trees for background planting are Red Oak (*Quercus rubra*), American Elm (*Ulmus americana*) and Sugar Maple (*Acer saccharum*). These trees are all so well known that a brief description will suffice. The Oak is, indeed, a majestic tree and well suited to any landscape subject. Downing sums up its chief characteristics in these few sentences: " There is a breadth about the lights and shadows reflected and embosomed in its foliage, a singular freedom and boldness in its outline and a pleasing richness and intricacy in its huge ramifications of branch and limb that render it highly adapted to landscape purposes." The Elm, while lacking something of the stateliness of the Tulip Poplar or the majesty of the Oak, outrivals them both in grace and elegance. The comparatively slender branches form into long, graceful curves until, in old trees, the light and airy foliage often sweeps the ground. The Elm should only be used when small groups are required. These trees, as a rule, are so similar in form as to be monotonous when planted together in large numbers. The Maple is valued for the rapidity of its growth, although it, too, has fine form and foliage. The Autumn coloring of the Sugar Maple, a beautiful, bright yellow, red and orange, is not equaled in any other tree.

FRAMING THE HOUSE

In addition to a suitable background it is essential that the residence be properly framed by plantations at both ends (Fig. 77). The size and character of this framework will depend largely on the architectural style and the dimensions of the house. For small houses, often one specimen tree, placed at each end, is quite sufficient. These lines from Milton will convey the picture of such a frame much better than a lengthy paragraph:

> " Hard by, a cottage chimney smokes
> From between two aged Oaks."

Houses built on a larger scale may require groupings. It is not always necessary nor advisable to plant the trees directly at the ends of the building. Usually a position forward of the front line gives a better effect.

TREES FOR FRAMING THE HOUSE

Where horizontal lines prevail in the general architectural scheme trees of a pyramidal type should be used. The Ginkgo (*Salisburia adiantifolia*), European Larch (*Larix europaea*) and Lombardy Poplar (*Populus fastigiata*) are good examples of such trees. The Ginkgo (Fig. 78) occasionally assumes a broad, spreading top, but this type is so infrequently met with that it may be, for all purposes, classed and used as a pyramidal tree. For planting near the house it is in a class alone and apart. Briefly, these

Fig. 78.—The Ginkgo, or Maidenhair Tree (Salisburia adiantifolia); a good type of pyramidal tree. "For planting near a house it is in a class alone and apart."—See page 80

Fig. 79.—The European Larch (Larix europæa); a splendid tree to use near houses where
horizontal lines predominate.—See page 84

Fig. 80.—The Cedrela (Cedrela sinensis). A good type of tree with spreading character; quick growing and free from insect attacks.—See page 84

are its chief attributes: Rapid growth, neat tapering head, unusual grayish bark, immunity from insects, beautiful leaves resembling greatly in form the leaves of the Maidenhair fern, and long life. The form and outline harmonize exceedingly well with buildings. The European Larch (Fig. 79) is a cone-bearing tree and belongs to the Pine family. It is not an evergreen, however, as it sheds its leaves in the Fall as do the deciduous trees. Perhaps its greatest charm is the picturesque appearance of even young trees. It has such an expression of boldness and freedom that, planted near the house, this effect must be relieved somewhat by grouping it with smaller harmonious trees, such as the White or Pink Dogwood (Fig. 3). The Lombardy Poplar in large quantities (Fig. 2) should be introduced only on large estates and to frame great houses. When planted near moderately sized dwellings the great height, often attained very quickly, is overwhelming.

When perpendicular lines predominate in the building the trees planted close to it should be of a spreading character unless for some particular reason the perpendicular lines are to be accentuated. We have a great variety of such trees to choose from. If the house is large the Red Oak, White Oak, Elm, Cedrela, Sugar Maple and Ash are equally good. The Cedrela (Fig. 80) is a Chinese tree resembling the Ailanthus, but without its objectionable features. It is rapid growing and generally desirable. Near medium or small houses the Scarlet Maple, Sweet Gum, European Linden, Yellow Wood and Oregon Maple all have the needed characteristics. The Oregon Maple is uncommon and should be more frequently planted. It somewhat resembles the Sycamore Maple, but is a more robust grower; it has a large, handsome, dark green leaf.

BASE PLANTINGS

Houses which set close to the ground should have no planting at the base. The turf should extend up to the lines of the porches or paved terrace, with group plantings at the corners.

Where the floor line is just enough above grade to admit of base plantings use plants dwarf in character (Fig. 81), with larger growing varieties at the corners and in the blank wall spaces between windows. An error to avoid is the planting of anything in front of window openings that will attain a height great enough to interfere with the light.

The outlines of base plantings should always be sinuous, extending out at the corners and receding to the face of the building. Where the width of the bed permits, the use of tall and low growing plants (Fig. 82) adds greatly to the effect from the approach.

WHAT TO AVOID IN BASE PLANTINGS

A popular practice today is the use of a miscellaneous assortment of evergreens in beds close to the house (Fig. 83). When the plants are small the effect is undoubtedly attractive and the contrast of the blue, green and golden foliage pleasing. Builders of suburban houses which it is desired to sell quickly have taken advantage of this appeal and, without thought of the future, have used these evergreen base plantings to the exclusion almost, in some communities, of the more desirable shrubbery groupings. This practice should not be followed in planting the home grounds. Many of the evergreens used are not dwarf types and soon outgrow their positions. The effect becomes monotonous in the extreme and lacks the variety of foliage, flower and fruit attainable by the use of a judicious selection of shrubs and broad-leaved evergreens.

PLANTS FOR BASE PLANTINGS—SHRUBS

A good selection of shrubs of a rather dwarf character can be made up from the following list: Spiræa Thunbergii, Spiræa Anthony Waterer, Deutzia gracilis, Caryopteris, Berberis Thunbergii, Azalea mollis, Desmodium penduliflorum, Deutzia Lemoinei, Daphne Mezereum, Forsythia suspensa, Spiræa arguta, Amygdalus nana, Ceanothus americana, Coriaria japonica, Hypericum aureum, Andromeda speciosa (Fig. 84). If the planting admits the use of larger growing plants these varieties are splendid for use close to the house: Spiræa Van Houttei, Rhodotypos kerrioides, Philadelphus Lemoinei, Neviusia alabamensis, Ligustrum Regelianum, Hydrangea paniculata grandiflora, Hydrangea arborescens grandiflora alba, Callicarpa purpurea, Weigela Eva Rathke.

PLANTS FOR BASE PLANTINGS—BROAD-LEAVED EVERGREENS

The broad-leaved evergreens are splendid for base plantings (Fig. 77), and will usually grow easily on any but a due southern exposure. The attractiveness of the foliage in Winter recommends them for liberal use in plantings near the house. Dwarf and tall growing kinds may be had in a diversity of form and foliage.

BASE PLANTINGS

Fig. 81.—" Where the floor line is just enough above the grade to admit of base plantings, use plants dwarf in character." Hardy shrubs provide more variety of foliage, flower and fruit than do the coniferous evergreens so often used.—See page 84

BASE PLANTINGS

Fig. 82.—We show a correct use of deciduous shrubs as a base planting. The outline of base plantings should always be sinuous, extending out at the corners and receding to the face of the building.—See page 85

AN INCORRECT BASE PLANTING

Fig. 83.—" A popular practice today is the use of a miscellaneous assortment of evergreens in beds close to the house."—See page 85

ILLUSTRATING USE OF SHRUBS IN BASE PLANTING

Fig. 84.—A good base planting of the larger growing shrubs. To complete the setting, two specimen trees, one at each end of the house, are needed to properly frame the dwelling.—See page 85

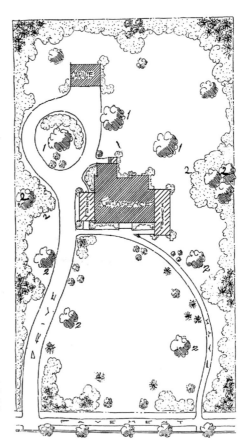

Fig. 85.—Plan showing a lawn planting around a small house. The trees marked No. 1 are placed for the purpose of a background, while those designated No. 2 are arranged for the framing of the residence. The belt plantation, shown in an irregular fashion, is more interesting and gives a greater variety to the scene than is possible with a straight border. Deciduous and evergreen trees are shown at the broad portions of the bed to give the necessary height and a more pleasing skyline.—See page 91

UNITY IS NOT IMPOSSIBLE ON SMALL PLANTINGS

Among the best are the Azaleas, the hybrid Rhododendrons, the Andromedas, Japanese Holly, Aucuba viridis, Kalmia latifolia, Laurocerasus, Abelia grandiflora, the Mahonias, Leucothoes and Phillyrea.

UNITY IN LAWN PLANTINGS

Between the house and the boundary lines lies that portion of the lawn which is most difficult to handle and the part that we usually find the least tastefully designed. On this part of the premises we have to consider plantings along drives, plantings along walks and paths, lawn specimens and lawn groups. These must be considered individually and yet so treated that with the background, plantings around the house, and boundary plantations, all will combine to produce a harmonious whole. This we speak of as unity. Unity is not impossible on small properties. It may be had by keeping the greensward open and confining the plantings to the borders and along the paths (Fig. 85). Attempt only the simple, if you will, just grass and trees, and the effect is much more pleasing than a large tract planted with no definite aim.

PLANTING FOR DETAIL

It is along the drives and paths that we may plant for the beautiful, as it is here that the observer is brought into closer touch with the individual plant and its every detail. Specimen plants for such plantations should have, therefore, some unusual and delicate characteristics, which would most likely be lost if placed at a greater distance from the eye. Among those which are most highly recommended are the cut-leaved White Birch, the various forms of the Japanese Maple, the fern-leaved Beech, and the Engligh Cork Maple. The Birch and the Maple are particularly handsome.

Specimens noted in previous paragraph, planted along the line of a drive, should be set back about fifteen or twenty feet so as to give them a little foreground (Fig. 86). The Japanese Maples are quite dwarf and may be planted closer. Allow each tree ample space for perfect development and allow for a stretch of greensward between specimens.

AVOID STRAIGHT LINES

The arrangement should be an avoidance of straight lines. The

PLANTING FOR DETAIL

Fig. 86.—Deciduous and evergreen trees, together with shrubbery, at the intersection of drive and pathway. The individual plants should be so planted that each will grow into a perfect specimen of its kind.—See page 91

larger growing trees should be near the house and the smaller kinds between the house and the entrance.   Large growing trees on a small lawn have a tendency to dwarf the area.   One or two large trees near the house will be quite sufficient in most cases.

AVOID ROWS OF TREES ALONG CURVED DRIVEWAYS

Lines of trees along curved driveways or paths should be dis-couraged. Groupings are much more artistic (Figs. 87 and 88). (See planting key, page 95.)

LINES OF TREES FOR STRAIGHT DRIVEWAYS

Along straight driveways lines of trees on either side are agreeable and are especially pleasing where they lead directly to the portals of the house, as is frequently seen on some of our old South-ern estates   The best trees for such purpose are the Sugar Maple, American Elm, Red Oak, and European Linden.   The trees should be planted alternately rather than directly opposite, and should be at least thirty-five feet apart, set back from five to ten feet from the edge of the drive; of the evergreens the White and Austrian Pines and the Norway Spruce are the most suitable.

SPECIMEN LAWN TREES

Specimen trees planted on the lawn should be low branched unless it is desirable to maintain a view under the overhanging limbs. Surface rooting trees, such as the soft or Silver Maple, should not be used, as it is difficult to maintain a lawn under them. The Oaks (Fig. 89) are deep rooted and almost unsurpassed as lawn specimens. The Sugar Maple, the large growing Magnolias, Kentucky Coffee, American Ash (Fig. 90) and English Ash, Sweet Gum and the Elms, are among the best deciduous trees. Specimen evergreens are greatly desirable and add to the Winter aspect. Such splendid trees as Nordmann's Fir, Cedar of Lebanon and Deodora Cedar (Fig. 91), Hemlock Spruce, Silver Fir, Blue Spruce (Fig. 92) and White Pine are among the most important.   If one has a love of trees, it is in the individual lawn specimens that a great variety may be had and, if care be used in the placing, the unity will still be preserved. As advised for specimen planting along drives, avoid straight lines. Keep the larger trees toward the back and do not crowd along the property line; place the smaller varieties toward the point of view.

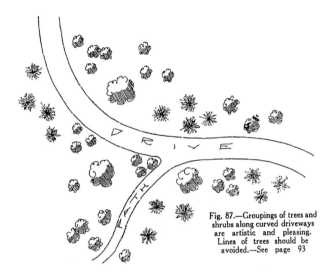

Fig. 87.—Groupings of trees and shrubs along curved driveways are artistic and pleasing. Lines of trees should be avoided.—See page 93

LAWN GROUPINGS

The lawn plantations or groups, those which are planted in the middle distance, should be pleasing in outline and so placed as to accentuate the view to some pleasing object beyond. The plants should be so arranged in the group that the outline is flowing and not stiff and regular. For the general arrangement and varieties best suited to such groupings we may take some suggestions from Nature, as there are certain trees and shrubs which we frequently find standing apart from woodlands.

The Balsam Fir and the White Birch (Fig. 93) make a pleasing combination planted together, also either the Austrian or White Pine and the Beech. The Oriental Spruce, Nordmann's Fir and Koster's Blue Spruce (Fig. 92) may be used together in groups with very gratifying results. The Japanese conifers, such as the Retinisporas, should always be grouped together or with the Arborvitæs. They do not harmonize well with the coarser leaved conifers.

KEY TO PLANTING PLAN.—Fig. 88.—A naturalistic planting along a curved driveway

Key No.	Quan.	Variety	Common Name
1	2	Quercus rubra	Red Oak
2	60	Rhodotypos kerrioides	White Kerria
3	3	Pinus sylvestris	Scotch Pine
4	60	Abelia grandiflora	Hybrid Abelia
5	2	Ulmus americana	American Elm
6	25	Viburnum tomentosum	Japanese Snowball
7	1	Acer saccharum	Sugar Maple
8	70	Lonicera Morrowi	Bush Honeysuckle
9	1	Pyrus floribunda	Flowering Crab
10	20	Crataegus Oxycantha	English Hawthorn
11	1	Juniperus Schottii	Schott's Cedar
12	1	Tsuga canadensis	Hemlock
13	70	Hydrangea quercifolia	Oak-leaved Hydrangea
14	1	Cerasus japonica rosea	Pink Japanese Cherries
15	1	Cedrela sinensis	Chinese Cedrela
16	40	Cercis canadensis	Red Bud
17	40	Buddleia Veitchii	Butterfly Plant
18	1	Thuya occi. pyramidalis	Pyramidal Arborvitae
19	1	Viburnum dilatatum	Japanese Bush Cranberry
20	50	Pyrus melanocarpa	Dwarf Pyrus
21	40	Cornus florida	White Dogwood
22	1	Betula lutea	Sweet Birch
23	30	Spirea Thunbergii	Snow Garland
24	3	Pterostyrax hispidum	Wistaria Tree
25	75	Jasminum nudiflorum	Yellow Jasmine
26	20	Cornus alternifolia	Blue Dogwood
27	135	Berberis Thumbergii	Japanese Barberry
28	40	Cornus mas.	Cornelian Cherry
29	1	Thuya occidentalis	Arborvitae
30	60	Viburnum acerifolium	Maple-leaved Viburnum
31	5	Crataegus Oxycantha	English Hawthorn
32	2	Pyrus Ionensis, Bechtel's Double-flowering	Bechtel's Crab
33	150	Hypericum Moserianum	St. John's Wort
34	60	Cotoneaster Simonsii	Shining Rose Box
34½	15	Caragana arborescens	Siberian Pea
35	3	Pinus Strobus	White Pine
36	70	Exochorda grandiflora	Pearl Bush
37	35	Xanthorrhiza apiifolia	Yellow Root
38	5	Pinus austriaca	Austrian Pine
39	75	Cercis japonica	Japanese Judas
40	1	Cedrela sinensis	Chinese Cedrela
41	1	Cornus florida	White Dogwood
42	75	Rosa humilis	Native Rose
43	1	Acer saccharum	Sugar Maple
44	1	Tsuga canadensis	Hemlock

Key No.	Quan.	Variety	Common Name
45	40	Berberis vulgaris	Common Barberry
46	40	Abelia grandiflora	Hybrid Abelia
47	20	Lonicera fragrantissima	Fragrant Honeysuckle
48	3	Pseudotsuga Douglasii	Douglas Fir
49	3	Quercus coccinea	Scarlet Oak

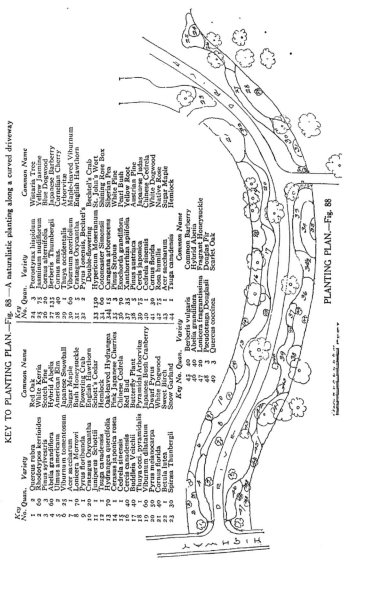

PLANTING PLAN.—Fig. 88.

ONE OF THE BEST TREES FOR THE LAWN

Fig. 89.—Pin Oak (Quercus palustris). Among other requirements, specimen lawn trees should be low branched. The Pin Oak fulfills every requirement.—See page 93

THE AMERICAN ASH MAKES A DESIRABLE SPECIMEN

Fig. 90.—American Ash (Fraxinus americana).   A quick growing type of desirable lawn
tree.—See page 93

A SUITABLE SPECIMEN TREE FOR SMALL LAWNS

Fig. 91.—Deodar Cedar (Cedrus Deodara).   Recommended as a specimen lawn tree.   Of
beautiful form and foliage; closely related to the Cedar of Lebanon.—See page 93

ALWAYS REMARKABLE AND ALWAYS DESIRABLE

Fig. 92.—Koster's Blue Spruce (Picea pungens Kosteriana). Well known as a desirable
evergreen; tips of foliage of a beautiful blue sheen.—See pages 93 and 94

Groups on small areas should not be overcrowded. If immediate effect is desired first arrange for the permanent trees and then
others may be added and removed as the desired trees develop. Individuals in group plantings should have ample space to show their
true characteristics, otherwise they assume a stiff, unnatural habit,
and mar the scene they are intended to embellish. It is a question
often as to just how much space some trees and shrubs require, so
great is the diversity in habit of growth. For the tall growing

THE BARK OF THE WHITE BIRCH OFFERS A PLEASING CONTRAST
Fig. 93.—The cut-leaved, pendulous White Birch (Betula alba laciniata pendula) is a good
tree for lawn groupings. With its white bark and graceful habit it lends itself to many
pleasing combinations.—See page 94

shrubs, such as the Weigela, Mock Orange, Snowball and Lilac, six feet apart is a good average; three feet will suffice for medium-sized plants; two feet for the dwarf growing kinds.   If these distances are followed it is advisable to set the plants in the turf and leave a space around each plant spaded up; when the grass dies out between the plants, the area may be made into a dug bed.   This system is much better than having a dug bed from the first with large, bare spaces between plants.   Should conditions favor the dug bed, a ground cover, such as Pachysandra, creeping Phlox, Candytuft, Rock Cress or Hypericum may be used to advantage.

PLANTING IN LAWN DEPRESSIONS

Where depressions occur in the lawn they may be accentuated by plantings on the slopes and high ground, leaving the depression open.

PLANTING IN VALLEYS

The view down a valley from the house site is always more restful if framed by plantings on the slopes.   In arranging the plants place the dwarfer kinds to the base and graduate the height to the top where the trees should predominate.

BOUNDARY PLANTINGS

Belt plantations (Fig. 94) are always appropriate where it is necessary to create the scene within the grounds or where privacy is desired.   When the surroundings are pleasingly planted or the natural conditions are such that the premises under consideration should be treated as a part of a general scheme, then the belt planting must not be continuous but broken to such an extent that it will blend harmoniously with what is already established.

Boundary or belt plantations (Fig. 95 on key page 104) should always be more or less sinuous, according to the area of the space we have to work with.   Even on the smallest properties the irregular compound curved line is more pleasing than a straight one.   The border should always be of greater depth at the corners, for it is here that we should have the greatest height.   On small properties the corner plantings become a part of the framework for the residence.   Where the area of the grounds is large the border may be extended well into the lawn at points and the bays thus formed will give an idea of greater distance looking from the house.

Border plantations are too frequently very regular and flat when shrubs alone are used (Fig. 96). The effect is especially displeasing when they stand out alone against the open with no background. It is well, therefore, to consider the skyline and introduce trees of various kinds at intervals. If the border is small choose the best of the dwarf sorts, and have the necessary height and variety of contour. In larger borders trees of greater dimensions should be used. A good choice may be made from among the following: Red Maple, Ash, Sugar Maple, Scarlet Oak and Sweet Gum. In addition to height and contour, all of these trees are noted for their splendid Autumn coloring.

Large growing trees introduced into the border make it necessary to select shade enduring shrubs to plant under and near them. For such a purpose use Aralia pentaphylla, Weigelas, Viburnum cassinoides, V. nudum, V. cotinifolium and V. acerifolium, Cornus alternifolia and C. paniculata, Hamamelis virginica, Ceanothus americana and broad-leaved evergreens (Fig. 97).

EDGING THE BORDER PLANTINGS

Edge the border planting with perennials, annuals and bulbs (Fig. 98), so that the season of bloom may be continuous from early Spring until late Fall. Keep away from bedding Tulips and other bulbs of a like nature in the border. Use Daffodils, Darwin Tulips and similar kinds that may be planted in clumps for naturalistic effect.

EVERGREENS IN BORDER PLANTINGS

If evergreens are used for a border planting set them in masses rather than as scattered specimens. Plant them in positions where it is desirable to have a Winter screen or where they will help plantings in front of them. If used as a background select only kinds that have green foliage. Plants, such as Judas, Golden Bell and Pyrus, together with shrubs having showy fruit, are very handsome against a background of evergreens (Fig. 99). The pyramidal type of evergreen, such as Arborvitæ, Cypress and Juniper, are highly recommended for border planting, as they give an accentuated note to the scene and add to the picturesqueness more than any other type of plant.

BOUNDARY PLANTINGS—Fig. 94.—"Belt plantations are always appropriate where it is necessary to create the scene within the grounds or where privacy is desired." Such plantations should always be more or less sinuous. Even on the smallest properties, the irregular curved line is more pleasing than a straight one. The combination of Spiræa Anthony Waterer and Yucca in this illustration is particularly good.—See page 101

PLANTING PLAN.   Fig. 95

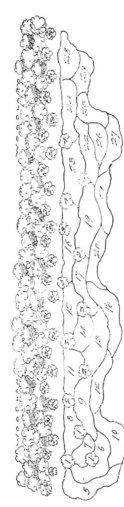

SCALE

KEY TO PLANTING PLAN   (Fig. 95).   BOUNDARY OR BELT PLANTATION

A belt planting along a woodland to make a break between the natural woodland and the lawn less abrupt.—See page 191

Key No.	Quan.	Variety	Common Name
1	3	Tsuga canadensis	Hemlock
2	3	Pinus austriaca	Austrian Pine
3	4	Pinus Strobus	White Pine
4	3	Tsuga canadensis	Hemlock
5	100	Berberis Thunbergii	Japanese Barberry
6	40	Viburnum dentatum	Arrow Wood
7	10	Euonymus alatus	Cork-barked Spindle Tree
8	25	Cercis canadensis	American Judas
9	25	Rhodotypos kerrioides	White Kerria
10	25	Ligustrum Regelianum	Regel's Privet
11	15	Cornus florida	White Dogwood
12	12	Cornus florida	Coral Berry
13	35	Symphoricarpos vulgaris	Snowberry
14	15	Symphoricarpos racemosus	Native Hydrangea
15	10	Hydrangea arborescens	Bush Honeysuckle
16	50	Lonicera tatarica	Varnish Tree
		Koelreuteria paniculata	Black Choke Berry
		Aronia melanocarpa	

Key No.	Quan.	Variety	Common Name
17	10	Lonicera fragrantissima	Early Honeysuckle
18	15	Crataegus cordata	Washington Thorn
19	30	Rubus odoratus	Flowering Bramble
20	30	Hydrangea arborescens grand. alba	Hills of Snow
21	30	Stephanandra flexuosa	Stephanandra
22	10	Cornus sericea	Silky Dogwood
23	10	Viburnum lentago	Sheepberry
24	10	Styrax japonica	Japanese Styrax
25	15	Vaccinium corymbosum	Cranberry
26	20	Rhodotypos kerrioides	White Kerria
27	30	Rhus copallina	Shining Sumach
28	15	Viburnum Opulus	High Bush Cranberry
29	25	Symphoricarpos vulgaris	Coral Berry
30	13	Cornus florida	White Dogwood
31	12	Cercis canadensis	Judas Tree

BORDER PLANTING ALONG A PROPERTY LINE

Fig. 96.—Instance of an attractive boundary planting along a property line, affording privacy and adding picturesqueness to the scene.—See page 102

SPECIMEN TREES IN FRONT OF BORDER PLANTINGS

Specimens planted in front of border plantings should always be at the salient points and not in the bays formed by the border outlines. The positions of specimen conifers should not be decided without reference to the border plants behind them. Evergreens with golden foliage should not be placed in front of shrubs with yellow leaves or flowers. Evergreens with blue foliage should not be placed in front of plants with silvery leaves. Strive to establish a contrast, but be careful to preserve good balance and harmony. If an existing plantation, either on the premises or beyond, consists of large trees, the specimens planted in the foreground should have foliage that will blend. Use trees of the same variety and depend for contrast on smaller trees and shrubs planted still more to the front.

AVOID ODD SHAPED BEDS IN LAWN CENTER

The center of the lawn surface should not be broken up with circular or geometrically shaped beds. They destroy the quietude and harmony of the scene.

ORNAMENTAL PLANTING ON THE FARM

While the farm layout should be thoroughly practical, the farmer who thinks that he must carry this so far that he can find no time or place for anything that is pleasing and beautiful around his residence, lining his highway, or even the field itself, is very wide of the mark. The average farm house of the past few decades and its collection of outbuildings have not been such as to inspire either respect, friendly sentiment or pleasant associations. The result has been that during the last fifty years our rural districts have lost greatly in population, the girls and boys of the farm finding more pleasure and enjoyment in the towns and cities.

The farm home and its surroundings should be made attractive and inspiring to the occupants, particularly to the younger generation, that they may see in their homes far more that is pleasant and enjoyable than in the tiny cubicles which pass for homes in our great cities.

It is not to be supposed that the farmer of average means can purchase fine paintings and works of art, but he can improve his

A MASS OF COLOR AT BLOOM TIME.—Fig. 97.—Rhododendrons in a border planting shaded by large trees.—See page 102

BORDER PLANTING EDGED WITH BULBS AND PERENNIALS
Fig. 98.—Ensuring continuous bloom from early Summer until late in Fall.—See page 102

immediate surroundings at very little cost, making the home a thing of beauty rather than a hideous collection of purely utilitarian conveniences.

The first aim in the landscape development should be toward an orderly arrangement of the barns, dairies, poultry yard and other features to be maintained for housing the stock and storing the crops. There is beauty as well as convenience in order. With the buildings located in their proper relation to each other and to the house, and the walk and drive arrangement carefully planned, the question of beautification is made quite simple.

All plantings should be composed of trees and shrubs that are very hardy and of easy culture, and for sentimental reasons it is well to select the old standard varieties familiar to old-time farms everywhere (Fig. 100).

Among the shrubs the most widely known is the Lilac. Lilacs are perfectly hardy and thrive in almost any soil and position. The varieties have been greatly improved, so that kinds may now be had with single or double flowers and in a wide range of color.

The Snowball is another favorite always found with the Lilac in the old-time farmyard. Other familiar kinds are the old-fashioned Sweet Shrub, Golden Bell, Bridal Wreath, Japanese Quince or Fire Bush, Mock Orange, Rose of Sharon and Weigelas. Add to these the Hydrangea and we have a selection that covers a long period of bloom.

There is not a place where these old-fashioned and greatly loved varieties may not be used to advantage as a means of ornamentation. Plant them at the corners of buildings, at fence corners, at interior angles, at intersections of walks and drives, and in pairs down the straight walk that leads to barn and garden.

The farm barn may have an end or side protected from the stock, which may be changed from an unsightly aspect to one of picturesqueness through the planting of a few hardy shrubs (Figs. 101, 102 and 103).

Although the truck garden is a strictly utilitarian feature, it is quite practical and not an extravagance to provide space for a small flower garden between the truck garden and the house, a sort of an anteroom to the strictly prosaic feature beyond.

The flower garden should not be large; it would be an error to make it so, and some of the space in the beds should be given over

PYRAMIDAL EVERGREENS IN BORDER PLANTINGS

Fig. 99.—Vervæne's Arborvitæ (Thuya occidentalis Vervæneana). A good type of pyramidal evergreen.—See page 102

ORNAMENTAL PLANTING ON THE FARM

Fig. 100.—A planting of old-fashioned shrubs around a farm house.—See page 109

A TYPE OF NEGLECT TOO OFTEN SEEN

Fig. 101.—Usual type of farm barn, entirely devoid of planting.—See page 109

QUITE DIFFERENT AND ALTOGETHER TO BE PREFERRED

Fig. 102.—An attractive planting of hardy trees and shrubs against the side of a farm barn. A constant pleasure to the farmer and his family.—See page 109

A FURTHER IDEA OF HOME GROUND IMPROVEMENT

Fig. 103.— Planting at the intersection of the highway and the road to the farm barn. It raises the value of farm property.—See page 109

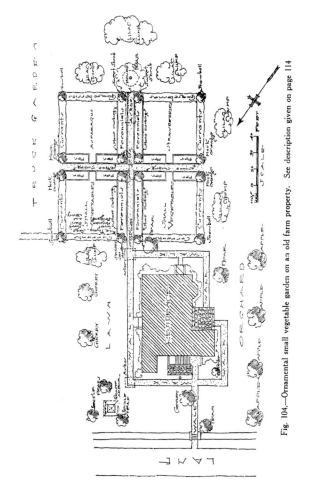

Fig. 104.—Ornamental small vegetable garden on an old farm property.   See description given on page 114

to the smaller vegetables and herbs, keeping the flower borders along the walks. In the old-time gardens these borders were defined by box edging or stone curbing. When stones were used they were whitewashed each Spring when the buildings and the fences receive their annual coat.

I recall a charming old garden which had been laid out along these lines (Fig. 104). The flower borders were four feet wide and the walks, of the same dimension, divided the area into four equal rectangles. On the axis of one of the walks, which was a continuation of a walk paralleling the front of the house, stood an old Catharine Pear, perched on a little mound, that formed a quiet resting place under the overhanging branches. The Pear was the center of the little lawn, about thirty feet square, partially enclosed by three clumps of Lilacs, and was the dominant note in the scene, standing stately and serene. At each corner of the garden and at the intersection of the walks were specimen shrubs, sixteen in all, and between them, back of the garden beds, were placed the Currant and Gooseberry bushes. In the flower beds were planted the herbs, and those old-fashioned garden favorites, Pæonies, Chrysanthemums, Larkspurs, Sweet Rockets, and Flags, preceded in the Spring by hundreds of yellow Daffodils, making a scene worthy of reproduction on every farm in the land.

SUMMARY

Briefly expressed, the use of ornamental trees and shrubs for the embellishment of a scene must be along lines that are both esthetic and practical. The selection of a particular plant or group of plants for a given position should be for the reason that it best suits that place, a point to be determined by a careful study of the best principles of landscape design. Simplicity and repose should be keynotes. Avoid the use of too many varieties and only as isolated specimens should abnormally shaped plants be admitted. Groups should consist of carefully selected units, all blending to make a pleasing whole.

From a practical viewpoint the success of any planting depends largely on the vigor and robustness with which the plants grow. Select plants best suited to the physical conditions in the locality. With splendid assortments to choose from in every section it is decidedly wrong to waste time and effort in trying to nurse along plants unsuited to local conditions.

TREE PLANTING

All plantings should be preceded by careful preparation of the soil. Lawn trees are permanent features and as such every detail of the planting should have close attention. This will insure a healthy growth and proper development.

Holes for trees should be at least a foot wider than the spread of the roots and at least twenty-four inches deep, unless for a large specimen, when it should be proportionately deeper.

In heavy clay soil, where the water is apt to collect and remain, the holes should be dug deep enough to afford good drainage. If the clay extends some depth proper drainage may be insured by placing broken stone in the bottom of the holes.

Tree holes should be made as large or larger at the bottom than they are at the top (Figs. 105 and 106). Too often holes just the reverse are prepared.

All broken or bruised roots should be cut off clean.

Holes should be sufficiently large to allow of spreading all roots in a natural position.

Good soil should be provided for the planting, and very dry and fine soil worked in carefully around the roots and thoroughly tamped so that no spaces remain.

Avoid planting too deeply (Fig. 107). Trees should be set just a very little lower than they have been growing in the nursery.

Avoid mounding up right around the stem after planting (Fig. 108). When this little hump gets dry and hard it makes a shed for that water which should penetrate to the roots.

A slight depression is much better and provides a cup for holding the moisture (Fig. 109). After planting, a good mulching over the root areas will conserve the moisture and greatly benefit the tree.

If the tree is three or five inches or more in caliper set wire stays to keep it straight and to protect against any loosening of the roots (Fig. 110).

PRUNING

The tops of all trees should be reduced at least one-third by pruning back when transplanting. This will overcome somewhat the loss of feeding roots and conserve the amount of sap in the trees until new feeding roots are formed.

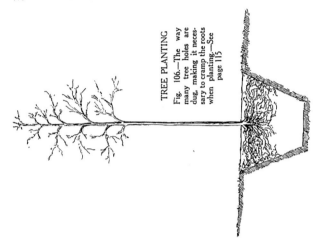

TREE PLANTING

Fig. 106.—The way many tree holes are dug, making it necessary to cramp the roots when planting.—See page 115

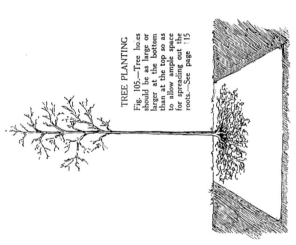

TREE PLANTING

Fig. 105.—Tree holes should be as large or larger at the bottom than at the top so as to allow ample space for spreading out the roots.—See page 115

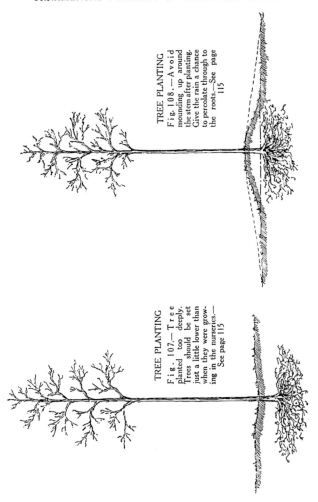

TREE PLANTING

Fig. 108.— Avoid mounding up around the stem after planting. Give the rain a chance to percolate through to the roots.—See page 115

TREE PLANTING

Fig. 107.— Tree planted too deeply. Trees should be set just a little lower than when they were growing in the nurseries.— See page 115

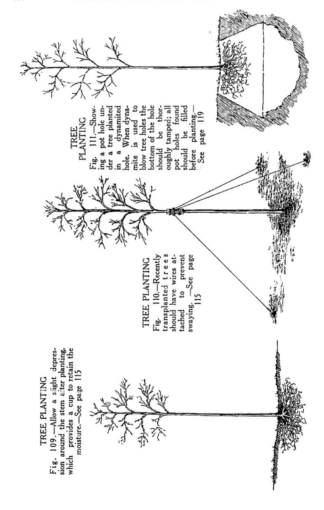

TREE PLANTING

Fig. 109.—Allow a slight depression around the stem after planting, which provides a cup to retain the moisture.—See page 115

TREE PLANTING

Fig. 110.—Recently transplanted trees should have wires attached to prevent swaying.—See page 115

TREE PLANTING

Fig. 111.—Showing a pot hole under a tree planted in a dynamited hole. When dynamite is used to blow tree holes the bottom of the hole should be thoroughly tamped; all pot holes found should be filled before planting.—See page 119

All such pruning should be done carefully, making the cuts clean and close up to a bud or stem, so that no stubs remain to die back and cause injury. Hard wooded trees such as the Oaks and Hickories must be cut back hard as they are apt to have fewer feeding roots than the softer wooded trees. Do not waste time and material on a poor specimen. Secure good, healthy trees with good root system and, if possible, trees that have been frequently transplanted.

TREE PLANTING WITH DYNAMITE

The blowing of tree holes with dynamite is to be recommended from the standpoint of economy alone. A good, big tree hole is much more easily dug if the ground has first been loosened with dynamite.

The loosening of the soil aids root growth and affords easy penetration of moisture to the root feeding areas.

One-half a stick of forty per cent. dynamite is usually sufficient for a hole.

One thing to avoid in planting trees in dynamited holes is the pot hole (Fig. 111), formed by the gases at the time of the explosion. Holes are not dug deeply enough after the explosion and this hole is allowed to remain. After a few rains have loosened the soil above it drops down to fill up the hole, leaving roots uncovered, often resulting in the loss of the tree. All dynamited holes should be gone over carefully with a long pole or bar so that the earth will settle into any deep holes that may have been formed.

MOVING LARGE TREES

On new estates quick results are often desired and may be secured by the planting of large specimen trees (Fig. 112).

The same principles apply to the moving of these large specimens as apply in all instances of tree transplanting. The trees must be carefully dug, preserving the small feeding roots even though they extend for a distance of from fifteen to twenty feet away from the trunk. As these are uncovered they should be tied up in bundles and bent out of the way, and protected with straw or burlap carefully wrapped around the roots.

If the trees are very large and heavy special apparatus must be secured for their proper handling.

The method of moving large trees with a six or eight foot ball of earth, cutting off all roots extending beyond, is not as satisfactory as tree moving where the roots are combed out and preserved.

ROOT PRUNING

When it is desired to move a large tree from one portion of the estate to another, the specimen should be root pruned at least one year in advance of the transplanting. This is accomplished by digging a trench about twelve inches wide, five or six feet away from the trunk, or a distance proportionate with the size of the tree, and filling the trench with soil and well-rotted manure to induce an added growth of small fibrous roots.

When moving large trees the head should be reduced somewhat to balance the loss in roots.

CARE OF TREES AND SHRUBS

Much of the beauty in plant life is in the healthy, vigorous growth, enabling the tree or shrub to put forth its best effort in pleasing foliage and abundant bloom and fruit. Continual and systematic attention should be given to the proper nourishing, watering and pruning of all trees and plants. The majority of our plants are existing under more or less unfavorable conditions and need this attention.

It plants are kept in a healthy, vigorous condition the susceptibility to insect, fungus, and scale attacks will be reduced to a minimum..

Trees planted in the lawn should have the sod removed from about them occasionally and a feeding of hardwood ashes, humus or well rotted manure applied. Such applications should extend to the area of the spread of the branches and not be confined to a very limited area immediately around the trunk.

When trees are kept mulched the mulching should be loosened occasionally to insure a free circulation of air.

All dead branches should be removed from trees, and all interfering limbs. This should be attended to at regular intervals. Neglect of proper pruning often causes irreparable damage to trees through heavy winds or ice storms.

All flowering shrubs should be properly and systematically pruned to insure an abundance of flower and fruit. Do not cut shrubs back during the Winter regardless of the variety or blooming season. Spring blooming shrubs, which of a necessity must form

LARGE TREES RECENTLY TRANSPLANTED

Fig. 112.—Showing immediate effect secured by using large trees. The Wier's Maple and the Elm were very recently transplanted.—
See page 119

flowering wood the season previous, should be pruned just after they have flowered. Lilacs, Golden Bell, Japanese Quince and similar Spring blooming shrubs are in this class. The pruning should not be too severe, simply enough to keep the plants in shape and to allow sunlight and air to all parts. The Fall flowering shrubs, such as the Rose of Sharon and Hydrangeas, bloom on wood made during the immediate Summer. · Such shrubs should have a vigorous Winter, or early Spring pruning.

INSECT PESTS

Insect pests attacking trees and shrubs are mostly of two kinds: those that injure by eating the foliage, such as the Elm Leaf Beetle, and those that injure by sucking, such as the various scales and plant lice.

For the leaf chewing insects a spraying with some poisonous substance that will readily adhere to the leaves is most effective. Paris green and arsenate of lead are recommended. These substances may be purchased in commercial form, prepared for such use, and accompanied by full instructions for proper application.

For scales and plant lice some remedy that kills by contact must be applied. Kerosene and soap emulsions are the best.

A wide band of burlap tacked around the tree with an overlap is very useful in arresting the progress of caterpillars. Such overlaps should be turned frequently and the caterpillars destroyed.

CHAPTER VII

THE FLOWER GARDEN

The highest personal note in the art of landscape design is the flower garden, and no scheme of landscape development is complete, no matter how small the property, which does not provide space for a garden. It is in the garden that our individual fancies as to the choice and arrangement of flowers may be indulged. There we may have a profusion of flowers, harmony of color, charm of effect and, above all, seclusion and restful quiet; for the growing of flowers is indeed the simplest yet most satisfying of pleasures.

We would emphasize again that fitness is the very foundation of all artistic excellence and in none of the arts is this more applicable than in garden design. The flower garden, although a separate unit in the general landscape, and subject in itself to a greater freedom of treatment, must be in harmony with its surroundings. If the house is of simple design simplicity must dominate the garden. That the charming box-bordered gardens of Colonial days were so in keeping with the residence was due largely to the simplicity of design—gardens with not only unpretentious outlines, but the variety of plants so limited that very simple color combinations resulted.

It is most gratifying to witness, since more attention is being given to the arrangement of the home surroundings, that the miscellaneous beds, which in former years were scattered over the lawn in a most heterogeneous fashion, are gradually being supplanted by the more orderly arrangement of plantations confined to the boundary lines of the property, bordered driveways or paths, or within enclosed areas, as formal or informal gardens.

CLASSIFICATION OF GARDENS

Enclosed gardens are by no means of modern origin. Space may not be given here to a full classification of various types of gardens, but it will be well to consider briefly those which have had great influence in the development of our present day garden. Of these, the Italian, French and English gardens are most important.

The Italian gardens did not depend on floral ornamentation for their chief beauty. While not entirely devoid of flowers they were mostly appreciated for their architectural embellishments.   Built upon three levels, ample opportunity was afforded for retaining walls, capped with balustrades of the most ornate character. The use of water in the garden was brought to its greatest perfection by the Italian architects. Remarkable water effects were achieved within a small compass and with little quantity.

The French gardens were also very architectural in design, but more extensive in area. Much consideration was given to vistas, particularly along diagonal lines. Many plants trimmed to formal outlines were used. Even the trees were treated as units in the architectural scheme, to be pruned and fashioned in harmony with the structural parts of the garden.

The Italian and French gardens, though softened by the elements of time and made interesting by the charm of romance, are not so satisfying as are the English gardens. The English garden exists more for its flowers and, although not devoid of architectural features, the masonry is softened by the abundant display of flowering plants. It is from the English garden and its flowers that we shall derive the greatest inspiration for our own gardens.

It is to the flower garden as an enclosed feature, of formal or informal design, that these notes will chiefly apply.

The flower garden should be treated as a unit in the general scheme and the principal views of the garden should be considered from the house. It should be an enclosure separated from the lawn by a wall or hedge. Such a scheme provides privacy and seclusion for those who would walk or work among the flowers; it is a protection to the growing plants and, in concealing this feature from without, leaves something to the imagination and more to be appreciated from a vantage point in the house.

GARDEN DIMENSIONS AND DESIGN

—GARDEN ENTRANCE

The principal entrance to the garden (Fig. 113) should be from the house and on an axis with some important door or window. It is from this point that we receive our first impression, and it should be so featured that the whole scene unfolded creates in the beholder that delight, fascination, allurement and complete sense of

Fig. 113.—Flower garden on the axis of the living room. All on one plane below the house level.—See page 124

rest which afford to lovers of nature the highest type of enjoyment. The garden should radiate an atmosphere of hospitality, creating an irresistible desire to stroll within and enjoy all the wealth of form and fragrance of foliage and flower.

The garden will always be more restful if placed on a level below the house grades (Figs. 114 and 114A), requiring steps for the descent.

Definiteness may be given to the garden entrance by an arch formed of plants in the enclosing hedge, or of metal or wood, framing some enticing water feature beyond.

Should it be necessary to place the garden on a higher level the approach should be broad and easy. Step risers should never be more than six inches and the tread should be at least fourteen inches.

The dimensions and shape of the garden are matters which will be influenced more or less by the residence and the configuration of the ground. The area of the garden, however, should always exceed that covered by the house. Where the property is rather narrow the greater dimension of the garden should extend in the direction of the greater dimension of the property.

When planning the garden the amount of care necessary for the proper upkeep should be borne in mind and the space designed accordingly, as it is necessary that the garden should at all times be in as nearly perfect condition as possible.

A flower garden adjoining a house should have some space between it and the house proper as the foreground to the floral scene beyond.

The rectangular design of beds in gardens possesses the greatest character and displays the plantations within the beds to the best advantage. This is specially so with the oblong enclosures. In square or nearly square gardens (Fig. 115), curved lines give a greater variety, especially within a small compass.

To add to the interest the design should always include a central feature, either a pool, bird bath, or even a sundial, although the latter is more appropriately placed in a more isolated position.

The central feature may be oblong, circular, elliptical, or a combination of the square and the circle.

In some instances it is advantageous, where the distance is not too great, to extend the garden from the house to the party line (Fig. 116—See page 136), arranging it so that it will come between the pleasure grounds and the service portion.

Fig. 114.—Garden on level below the house terrace.—See page 126.   Fig. 114A—(Pages 128, 129) shows planting plan of this garden.

KEY TO PLANTING PLAN.—Fig. 114A—See pages 130 and 131

Key No.	Quan.	Variety	Common Name
1	8	Aconitum Napellus	Monkshood
2	10	Delphinium chinense	Chinese Larkspur
3	9	Pentstemon barbatus hybrids	Beard's Tongue
4	10	Gypsophila acutifolia	Baby's Breath
5	15	Coreopsis lanceolata	Tickseed
6	7	Helenium Hoopesii	Early Sneezewort
7	7	Aconitum Napellus	Monkshood
8	5	Achillea, The Pearl	Double White Yarrow
9	6	Phlox, Miss Lingard	Early Phlox White
10	6	Phlox Sieboldi	Tall Vermilion Phlox
11	7	Aconitum Napellus	Monkshood
12	12	Lupinus polyphyllus	Lupine
13	6	Aster lævis	Lavender Hardy Aster
14	5	Hollyhocks Allegheny	Fringed Hollyhocks
15	7	Aster novæ angliæ rosea	Pink Hardy Aster
16	11	Delphinium elatum	Tall Larkspur
17	8	Anchusa Italica Dropmore var.	Alkanet
18	11	Physostegia virginica	Obedient Plant
19	10	Delphinium elatum	Tall Larkspur
20	10	Delphinium elatum	Tall Larkspur
21	5	Boltonia latisquama	Starwort
22	8	Anchusa Italica Dropmore var.	Alkanet
23	7	Delphinium elatum	Tall Larkspur
24	7	Aster novi belgii climax	Pink Hardy Aster
25	7	Hollyhocks Allegheny	Fringed Hollyhocks
26	10	Heliopsis Pitcheriana	Orange Sunflower
27	9	Aconitum Napellus	Monkshood
28	7	Phlox, Miss Lingard	Early Phlox, white
29	5	Phlox, Rheinlander	Salmon Pink Hardy Phlox
30	5	Phlox Sieboldi	Vermilion Hardy Phlox
31	11	Aconitum Napellus	Monkshood
32	11	Chrysanthemum Golden Mme. Martha	Yellow Hardy Chrysanthemum
33	5	Aster lævis	Lavender Hardy Aster
34	9	Hollyhocks, double red	Double Red Hollyhocks
35	10	Aquilegia chrysantha	Yellow Columbine
36	11	Phlox W. C. Egan	Light Lavender Phlox
37	13	Chrysanthemum St. Illoria	Pink Hardy Chrysanthemum
38	10.	Phlox Queen	White Phlox
39	2	Juniperus Cannarti	Pyramidal Cedar
40	2	Juniperus Pfitzeriana	Spreading Cedar
41	2	Juniperus Cannarti	Pyramidal Cedar
42	12	Dianthus barbatus Newport Pink	Pink Sweet William
43		Godetias (annual)	
44	6	Campanula persicifolia	Peach-leaved Bellflower
45	7	Iris aurea	Yellow Flag
46	5	Gypsophila paniculata	Baby's Breath
47	9	Digitalis purpurea	Foxglove
48	5	Aquilegia cærulea	Rocky Mountain Columbine
49	9	Phlox amœna	Early Phlox Pink
50	5	Pentstemon barbatus	Beard's Tongue
51	7	Sedum spectabile	Live Forever
52	9	Aquilegia chrysantha	Yellow Columbine
53	3	Chrysanthemum Julia Lagravère	Red Hardy Chrysanthemum
54	5	Phlox Baron von Dedem	Red Hardy Phlox
55	4	Calliopsis (annual)	
56	5	Anemone Japonica Queen Charlotte	Pink Japanese Anemone
57	5	Papaver orientale	Oriental Poppy
58	5	Doronicum excelsum	Leopard's Bane
59	7	Delphinium chinense alba	White Chinese Larkspur
60	12	Phlox Independence	White Hardy Phlox
61	7	Phlox Coquelicot	Scarlet Hardy Phlox
62	7	Dianthus barbatus, white	White Sweet William
63	7	Gaillardia grandiflora	Blanket Flower

KEY TO PLANTING PLAN.—Fig. 114A—Continued

Key No.	Quan.	Variety	Common Name
64	7	Chrysanthemum Golden Mme. Martha	Golden Chrysanthemum
65	5	Sedum spectabile " Brilliant "	Live Forever
66	7	Coreopsis lanceolata	Tickseed
67	9	Phlox amœna	Early Pink Phlox
68	5	Iris Kæmpferi	Japanese Iris
69	7	Gypsophila elegans	Baby's Breath
70	7	Aquilegia canadensis	Red Columbine
71	5	Dianthus Newport Pink	Pink Sweet William
72	7	Dianthus barbatus white	White Sweet William
73	5	Coreopsis lanceolata	Tickseed
74	5	Chrysanthemum Autumn Queen	Pink Hardy Chrysanthemum
75	5	Dianthus Newport Pink	Pink Sweet William
76	7	Rudbeckia Newmanni	Black-eyed Susan
77	9	Gaillardia grandiflora	Blanket Flower
78	3	Heuchera sanguinea	Coral Bells
79	10	Gypsophila paniculata	Baby's Breath
80	7	Phlox divaricata	Early Blue Phlox
81	5	Veronica longifolia subsessilis	Speedwell
82	10	Delphinium elatum	Tall Larkspur
83	10	Gypsophila paniculata	Baby's Breath
84	5	Aster amellus elegans	Early Aster
85	5	Platycodon grandiflorum	Bellflower
86	5	Aconitum Napellus	Monkshood
87	5	Delphinium chinense	Chinese Larkspur
88	5	Pentstemon Torreyi	Beard's Tongue
89	7	Lupinus polyphyllus	Lupine
90	5	Scabiosa japonica	Blue Bonnet
91	7	Delphinium, Gold Medal Hybrids	Tall Larkspur
92	5	Aster novi belgii Heiderose	Hardy Aster
93	5	Iris pallida dalmatica	Lavender Iris
94	5	Coreopsis lanceolata grandiflora	Tickseed
95	3	Campanula glomerata	Clustered Bellflower
96	7	Iris Kæmpferi	Japanese Iris
97	7	Phlox divaricata	Early Blue Phlox
98	5	Delphinium elatum	Tall Larkspur
99	7	Veronica longifolia subsessilis	Speedwell
100	12	Rose Christine Wright	Climbing Pink Rose
101	5	Stokesia cyanea	Stoke's Aster
102	5	Gypsophila paniculata	Baby's Breath
103	7	Aquilegia vulgaris	Columbine
104	7	Phlox Miss Lingard	Early White Phlox
105	7	Centaurea montana	Hardy Cornflower
106	5	Dianthus plumarius	Snow Queen
107	7	Iris pallida dalmatica	Lavender Flag, White, Pink
108	5	Dianthus plumarius Homer	Hardy Pink
109	10	Plumbago Larpentæ	Leadwort
110	5	Platycodon grandiflorum	Bellflower
111	5	Coreopsis grandiflora	Tickseed
112	9	Iris Kæmpferi	Japanese Iris
113	12	Aster blue (annuals)	
114	3	Pæonia l'Esperance	Pink Peony
115	5	Funkia cærulea	Blue Day Lily
116	10	Delphinium formosum	Tall Larkspur
117	12	Lilium candidum	Madonna Lily
118	5	Potentilla Vulcan	Crimson Cinquefoil
119	7	Chrysanthemum Autumn Queen	Pink Chrysanthemum
120	7	Aquilegia vulgaris	Columbine
121	8	Dianthus barbatus, white	Sweet William
122	5	Delphinium chinense	Chinese Larkspur
123	10	Geum coccineum	Avens
124	10	Plumbago Larpentæ	Leadwort
125	5	Platycodon grandiflorum	Bellflower
126	9	Dianthus plumarius Homer	Hardy Pink
127	7	Coreopsis grandiflora	Tickseed
128	10	Iris Kæmpferi	Japanese Iris
129	7	Iris pallida dalmatica	Lavender Flag
130	10	Lilium candidum	Madonna Lily
131	10	Delphinium flormosum	Dark Blue Larkspur
132	10	Potentilla Vulcan	Crimson Cinquefoil

GARDENING

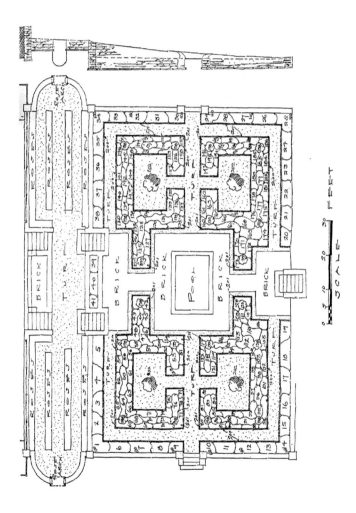

KEY TO PLANTING PLAN.—Fig. 114A—Continued

Key No.	Quan.	Variety	Common Name
133	7	Aquilegia vulgaris	Columbine
134	5	Funkia ovatus	Blue Day Lily
135	9	Dianthus barbatus	Sweet William
136	9	Chrysanthemum Autumn Queen	Pink Hardy Chrysanthemum
137	5	Linum perenne	Hardy Flax
138	7	Centaurea montana	Hardy Cornflower
139	7	Delphinium elatum	Tall Larkspur
140	10	Aquilegia vulgaris	Blue Columbine
141	10	Gypsophila paniculata	Baby's Breath
142	10	Clematis Davidiana	Perennial Clematis
143	5	Veronica longifolia subsessilis	Speedwell
144	10	Phlox divaricata	Early Blue Phlox
145	7	Campanula Dahurica	Bellflower
146	6	Stokesia cyanea	Stoke's Aster
147	5	Coreopsis longifolia grandiflora	Tickseed
148	5	Aster lævis	Hardy Aster Lavender
149	5	Delphinium, Gold Medal Hybrids	Tall Larkspur
150	7	Lupinus polyphyllus	Lupines
151	7	Pentstemon barbatus hybrids	Beard's Tongue
152	8	Iris pallida dalmatica	Lavender Flag
153	11	Platycodon grandiflorum	Japanese Bellflower
154	5	Aconitum Napellus	Monkshood
155	10	Scabiosa japonica	Blue Bonnet
156	9	Delphinium elatum	Tall Larkspur
157	10	Gypsophila paniculata	Baby's Breath
158	7	Veronica longifolia subsessilis	Speedwell
159	5	Delphinium chinense	Chinese Larkspur
160	7	Phlox amœna	Early Pink Phlox
161	5	Sedum spectabile	Live Forever
162	10	Geum coccineum	Avens
163	10	Aquilegia chrysantha	Yellow Columbine
164	5	Chrysanthemum Julia Lagravère	Red Chrysanthemum
165	9	Pentstemon barbatus	Beard's Tongue
166	8	Phlox Rheinstrom	Salmon Pink Hardy Phlox
167	10	Gypsophila paniculata	Baby's Breath
168	10	Digitalis purpurea	Foxgloves
169	9	Iris Kæmpferi	Japanese Iris
170	10	Iris aurea	Yellow Flags
171	5	Chrysanthemum Gólden Mme. Martha	Golden Chrysanthemum
172	10	Dianthus Newport Pink	Pink Sweet William
173	7	Aquilegia chrysantha	Yellow Columbine
174	7	Papaver orientale	Oriental Poppy
175	7	Delphinium chinense alba	White Chinese Larkspur
176	5	Anemone japonica Queen Charlotte	Pink Japanese Anemone
177	7	Doronicum excelsum	Leopard's Bane
178	5	Phlox Coquelicot	Scarlet Phlox
179	9	Digitalis purpurea alba	White Foxglove
180	11	Gaillardia grandiflora	Blanket Flower
181	10	Dianthus barbatus, white	Sweet William
182	10	Gladiolus Wm. Falconer	
183	5	Chrysanthemum Golden Mme. Martha	Golden Chrysanthemum
184	5	Sedum spectabile	Live Forever
185	9	Coreopsis lanceolata	Tickseed
186	9	Phlox amœna	Dwarf Early Pink Phlox
187	5	Iris Kæmpferi	Japanese Iris
188	7	Gypsophila paniculata	Baby's Breath
189	7	Aquilegia canadensis	Red Columbine
190	5	Chrysanthemum Autumn Queen	Pink Hardy Chrysanthemum
191	7	Dianthus barbatus, white	Sweet William
192	5	Coreopsis grandiflora	Tickseed
193	7	Gaillardia grandiflora	Blanket Flower
194	7	Pæonia Van Houttei	Peony
195	5	Rudbeckia fulgida	Black-eyed Susan
196	7	Heuchera sanguineum	Coral Bells
197	10	Gypsophila paniculata	Baby's Breath
198	12	Buxus pyramidalis	Pyramidal Box, 4-5'
199	8	Juniperus Cannarti	Pyramidal Cedar, 4-5'
200	3000	Dwarf Box for edging	6-8"
201	48	Tall Pink Geraniums	
202	4	Cratægus Oxycantha	Standard Eng. Hawthorn, 6" stems

The entire garden area should be on one plane if it is possible to so construct it at not too great an expense. This level should be somewhat below the established grade of the house line (Fig. 113). Where the slope of the ground is too steep for such treatment, two or three levels may be established. A garden constructed on different levels may be made very interesting, as it affords an opportunity to introduce many architectural features and to vary greatly the planting on the different planes.

GARDEN BACKGROUND

It is important to consider the garden from the picturesque point of view. This will include not only the arrangement of the interior beds but, quite as important, the setting of the surrounding plantations. The background (Fig. 117) should be dense, of a varied assortment of plants. Where space permits, and the height of the plants will not interfere with the view, make a background of White Pine, Hemlock, Birch, Beech, Maple and Ash. Such a combination will give pleasing contrast at all seasons of the year, especially in the Fall, when the foliage of the deciduous trees turns to brilliant shades of red and yellow. On extensive grounds such a background planting may be placed some distance from the garden and particularly so when there is a little rise in the ground beyond the end of the garden.

When the garden area extends to the party line it is necessary to provide a high hedge or wall which will rise above the horizon. If a wall is used it should be partly clothed with vines as green is the most satisfactory garden background (Fig. 118). It is possible sometimes to so locate the garden that a natural background on the adjoining property may be taken advantage of.

A pleasing effect may often be secured in gardens enclosed by a wall, by introducing flowering trees and shrubs in the plantations immediately without, so that the branches may be trained to hang over the wall to meet the floral ensemble within.

GARDEN ENCLOSURES

The garden in the sense that it is used in these paragraphs refers to a portion of the estate set aside as an enclosed feature. An enclosure provides privacy and seclusion to those who would walk or work among the flowers; it is a protection to the growing plants,

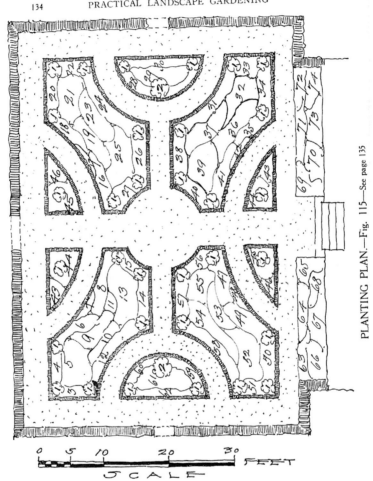

PLANTING PLAN.—Fig. 115—See page 135

"In square or nearly square gardens curved lines give a greater variety, especially within a small compass"

KEY TO PLANTING PLAN.—Fig. 115

Fig. 115.—In a square or a nearly square garden curved lines give greater variety, especially within a small compass.—See planting plan, page 134, also page 126

Key No.	Quan.	Variety	Common Name	Key No.	Quan.	Variety	Common Name
1	32	Buxus arborescens pyramidalis	Pyramidal Box	37	12	Delphinium formosum	Indigo Larkspur
2	2	Thuya occidentalis globosa	Globe Arborvitæ	38	16	Aster, blue	Annual Aster
3	12	Vinca rosea alba	White Madagascar Periwinkle	39	14	Phlox tapis blanc	Semi-dwarf White Phlox
4	12	Phlox divaricata	Early Blue Phlox	40	10	Antirrhinum, white	Snapdragon
5	20	Stokesia cyanea	Stokes Aster	41	12	Veronica longifolia subsessilis	Early Phlox
6	12	Iris Blue Boy	Blue Flag	42	6	Veronica longifolia subsessilis	Speedwell
7	6	Veronica longifolia subsessilis	Speedwell	43	12	Petunia, single white	Petunia
8	12	Phlox Ardensi, Amanda	Early Phlox	44	12	Heliotrope Chieftain	Heliotrope
9	12	Delphinium formosum	Indigo Larkspur	45	12	Heliotrope Chieftain	Heliotrope
10	8	Chrysanthemum Sœur Melaine	White Hardy Chrysanthemum	46	12	Petunia, single white	Petunia
11	4	Platycodon grandiflora	Bellflower	47	20	Verbena, pink	Verbena
12	30	Ageratum Blue Perfection	Painter's Brush	48	12	Viola, White Perfection	Tufted Pansy
13	14	Phlox Von Lassburg	White Phlox	49	20	Calendula sulphurea	Pot Marigold
14	16	Aster, blue	Annual Aster	50	15	Calliopsis	Annual Coreopsis
15	10	Antirrhinum, white	Snapdragon	51	15	Petunia, single white	Petunia
16	20	Verbena, pink	Verbena	52	15	Chrysanthemum Globe d'Or	Hardy Chrysanthemum
17	7	Iberis sempervirens	Candytuft	53	10	Helenium Hoopesii	Early Sneezewort
18	12	Calendula sulphurea	Pot Marigold	54	16	Chrysanthemum St. Iloria	Pink Chrysanthemum
19	16	Phlox Ardensi Grete	Early Phlox	55	14	Phlox, Elizabeth Campbell	Pink Hardy Phlox
20	6	Gaillardia grandiflora	Blanket Flower	56	7	Antirrhinum, pink	Snapdragon
21	18	Chrysanthemum Globe d'Or	Yellow Hardy Chrysanthemum	57	12	Chrysanthemum arcticum	Arctic Daisy
22	15	Petunia, single white	Petunia	58	30	Centaurea imperialis, pink	Sweet Sultan
23	10	Helenium Hoopesii	Early Sneezewort	59	15	Viola, White Perfection	Tufted Pansy
24	30	Centaurea imperialis, pink	Sweet Sultan	60	15	Petunia, white	Petunia
25	15	Phlox Elizabeth Campbell	Pink Phlox	61	20	Heliotrope Chieftain	Heliotrope
26	12	Chrysanthemum arcticum	Arctic Daisy	62	20	Arctotis	African Daisy
27	10	Antirrhinum, pink	Pink Snapdragon	63	12	Aquilegia chrysantha	Yellow Columbine
28	20	Dimorphotheca aurantiaca	Orange Daisy	64	15	Aster alpina	Alpine Aster
29	20	Antirrhinum, yellow	Snapdragon	65	10	Funkia cærulea	Plantain Lily
30	20	Verbena, white	Verbena	66	15	Lupinus polyphyllus	Lupine
31	30	Ageratum Blue Perfection	Painter's Brush	67	15	Phlox Von Lassburg	White Phlox
32	15	Stokesia cyanea	Stokes' Aster	68	6	Delphinium formosum	Indigo Larkspur
33	12	Vinca rosea alba	White Madagascar Periwinkle	69	8	Funkia cærulea	Plantain Lily
34	8	Phlox divaricata	Blue Early Phlox	70	8	Pentstemon Torreyi	Beard's Tongue
35	15	Chrysanthemum Sœur Melaine	White Chrysanthemum	71	20	Viola lutea splendens	Tufted Pansy
		Iris pallida dalmatica	Lavender Flag	72	10	Chrysanthemum arcticum	Arctic Daisy
				73	12	Aster, tall white	Annual Aster
				74	8	Phlox Elizabeth Campbell	Pink Hardy Phlox

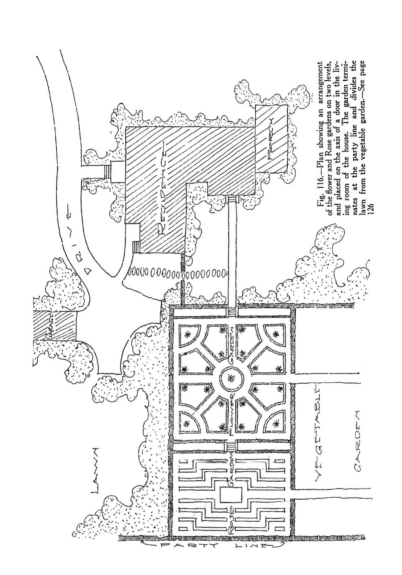

Fig. 116.—Plan showing an arrangement of the flower and Rose gardens on two levels, and placed on the axis of a door in the living room of the house. The garden terminates at the party line and divides the lawn from the vegetable garden.—See page 126

Fig. 117.—A very pretty garden below the house line, simple in outline and so located as to have the advantage of a wooded background. The bay trees and pyramidal conifers lift it up and give variety to an otherwise uninteresting skyline. The view to the figure is enhanced through the introduction of these larger plants. It is preferable to have them planted in the ground rather than in tubs.—See page 133

affords a background and, in concealing the garden from without, leaves something to the imagination and more to be appreciated from a vantage point in the house.

Garden enclosures may be of stone, brick, stucco or plants in the form of a hedge.

HEIGHT OF GARDEN ENCLOSURES

The height of outer garden enclosures will vary according to the surroundings. Where the outlook is not particularly attractive they may be six or seven feet high. High walls are also a necessity in some localities as a protection to the plants. Where it is thought best to maintain views of the surrounding landscape a wall three to five feet high is sufficient. Subordinate garden walls should not be more than three to four feet high. On a small place, where the scene must be made within the enclosure, a high wall is necessary.

GARDEN WALLS

When walls are adopted as an enclosure for the garden they should always be of the same material as the house. If the house walls are stuccoed the sides of the garden wall should also be stuccoed, though, to provide a slight contrast, the piers and coping may be of brick. This refers to gardens which are adjacent to residences. When they are set apart, more or less isolated from the house, the material may differ from that in the building.

When walls of stone, brick, or stucco are used for the garden enclosures they should be designed along artistic lines and be in perfect harmony with the scene to be created.

GRAY SANDSTONE WALLS

Soft gray sandstone (Fig. 118) with an occasional marking of red and orange is the most pleasing stone for the enclosing walls. These should not be less than eighteen inches thick with a footing course to project six inches beyond on each side, making a thickness of thirty inches. The depth of the footing should not be less than eight inches. The depth of the foundation below the frost line will depend on the latitude. In Philadelphia and vicinity the foundation should extend to a depth of three feet.

Fig. 118.—The natural background on an adjoining property makes a good setting for the garden. Gray sandstone enclosing walls with similar coping stone.—See pages 133, 138, 140 149

Stone walls with mortar joints should be less finished in texture than the house walls. The joints should be raked out to a depth of from two to three inches. The shadows produced by this treatment have a softening effect and the vines, extending their clinging tendrils into the interstices, seem to be more firmly fixed to the supporting structure.

COPING

The coping should be of stone similar to that in the body of the wall (Fig. 118), with a projection of two to three inches, according to the roughness of the face. This refers to a coping of stones laid flat. If the coping stones are set on edge they should be set flush with the sides of the wall. The coping should be level along the top.

The irregular or so-called scotched coping is not at all satisfactory for a garden enclosure, as it is a line of agitation and most unrestful.

BRICK WALLS

The brick wall (Fig. 119) as a garden enclosure is not so pleasing from an esthetic point of view as those of other materials. Because of the color it does not make a good background for many of the flowers. If brick is used a dark shade should be selected and laid with a broad mortar joint.

A brick wall should not be less than twelve inches thick and should be laid in cement mortar on a good foundation of stone or concrete extending not less than four inches on each side beyond the face of the finished wall. To economize on a quantity of brick the wall may be paneled and piers placed at intervals of from ten to twelve feet apart, using a nine-inch wall between them.

An effective and practical wall may be constructed by laying the brick lengthwise, four inches thick, with a two-inch opening between the ends. In this construction the piers should be placed eight feet apart.

The coping for a brick wall may be of brick on edge, molded brick, brick laid on an angle of 45 degrees, cement cut stone, or tile. The coping should have a projection of not more than an inch on each side of the wall. A coping set flush is quite agreeable. All brick walls should be clothed with clinging vines trained over the top to break the line and soften the effect.

Fig. 119.—Brick garden wall with an attractive entrance treatment.—See page 140

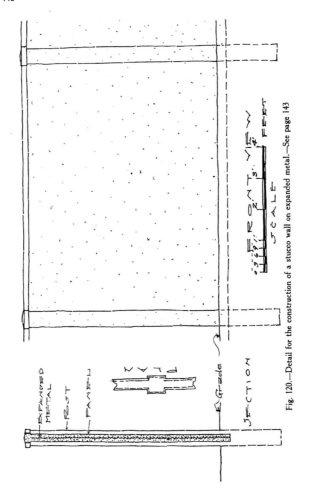

Fig. 120.—Detail for the construction of a stucco wall on expanded metal.—See page 143

THE STUCCO WALL

The stucco wall may be laid on stone, brick, hollow tile, or expanded metal. The usual method is to construct a rough wall on which is laid the first or scratch coat. When this has very nearly set a second coat of the color and texture desired is applied and finished.

If the rough wall is built of brick it should not be less than nine inches thick, with a firm foundation of eighteen to twenty inches of stone or concrete, extending below the frost line usually from two to three feet.

When building a stucco wall on brick a good effect may be secured by having a brick base and brick coping. The base to consist of a row of brick on end, projecting one quarter inch beyond the finished mortar surface. The coping should be constructed of a row of brick on edge with a very slight projection on each side of the wall.

If hollow tile is used for the rough wall eight-inch tile may be used for walls less than five feet high; for walls above that, twelve inch tiles should be used.

The brick base and coping may be effectively used with the hollow tile. Foundation should be the same as is used for brick.

Rough stone walls for stucco should not be less than sixteen inches thick for walls five feet high or less. For walls above five feet the thickness should be at least eighteen inches. Foundation should be of stone or concrete, twenty to twenty-two inches thick and extending below the frost line.

The most economical stucco wall is that laid on expanded metal (Fig. 120) supported by channel iron set at intervals of one foot, with four channel irons set at intervals of eight feet in the form of a square, six inches apart, as a reinforcement. The cement mortar is worked through the openings in the expanded metal and, after it becomes hardened, the scratch coat is applied to the other side, the mortar clinging to the keys formed by the mortar worked through the openings. The finish coat of the texture and finish desired is then applied.

The posts for such a wall should extend to a depth of two feet and be set in concrete. For the remainder of the wall it is only necessary to have the mortar extend six inches below the grade line.

The coping should be of mortar two and one-half inches thick, beveled on top, with a projection of about one-half inch on each side. All stucco walls should be covered with quick growing vines. Boston Ivy (*Ampelopsis Veitchii*), Red-berried Euonymus (*Euonymus vegetus*), and English Ivy (*Hedera helix*) are suitable.

DRY STONE WALLS

The rubble stone wall of field boulders is most satisfactory, and, when partly covered by vines, is highly picturesque. The dry wall may also be used to enclose the garden, especially in locations where good rock is to be had on the ground. When used for this purpose they should batter or break back from each side, vines to be planted along the full length at irregular intervals. The vines should not be allowed to cover the entire wall. Rather, for reasons of contrast, and to show decidedly the limitations of the garden and the formidableness of the retaining and supporting walls, quite good stretches of it should be left uncovered.

Rubble walls (Fig. 121) are particularly good where a retaining wall is required to maintain an embankment. The dry wall is less expensive than one laid in mortar and gives a greater latitude for ornamental treatment. Quarried stone or stone gathered on the property may be used for this purpose. The larger the stones the better. If the stones are from a quarry they should be as long as it is possible to secure them.

The dry wall should have a batter of not less than one inch to the foot, and where it is proposed to use Alpine plants in the interstices it is better to have a batter of three inches to the foot. The building of a dry wall for plants is given in greater detail in the chapter on Rock Plants.

HEDGES

The hedges of various plants are much less expensive and fulfil many requirements as a dividing line between lawn and garden. The Privet hedge is the most popular, as its quick growth and dark green leafage form an excellent background in a short period of time. The California Privet (*Ligustrum ovalifolium*), which is most frequently used, is not hardy in some latitudes; the tops are occasionally killed to the ground in Philadelphia, and instances are reported of the same damage being done in Kentucky. For cold latitudes the variety Ligustrum Ibota is more satisfactory. The

Fig. 121.—Retaining walls in the garden. How much more effective is this treatment than the slope generally adopted when the garden is on more than one level.—See pages 144, 146

Ligustrum Regelianum is an excellent hedge plant where it is desired to have a more picturesque enclosure. This plant is most attractive as a boundary to a wild garden, the lights and shadows being highly contrasted, giving a pleasing variety to this formal feature more in tune with naturalistic surrounding. The variety Ligustrum amurense is much the best variety to use south of Washington; it rarely loses its leaves during the Winter and, in the Carolinas, Tennessee and Georgia it is evergreen.

The Hemlock Spruce (*Tsuga canadensis*) (Fig. 122) hedge has been little used of late years, probably on account of its costliness, certainly not because it lacks beauty of outline or texture. The color is excellent as a background and, after growing to the required height, it is much more formidable in appearance than the deciduous hedges. For quick effect the Arborvitæ (*Thuya occidentalis*) is most valuable. It is practicable to secure specimens of this variety of any height up to seven feet, which is an advantage for instances where it is desired to have an immediate effect. The color is not so good for a background as plants of a darker shade of green but, nevertheless, is recommended as a hedge plant of merit.

The general character of the garden will be improved by using piers at the corners and entrance. It adds dignity to the scenes and defines the outline more clearly. In large gardens, where a long line of hedge is somewhat monotonous and at times irregular in alignment, it is well to construct piers at regular intervals, for variety, and to maintain a more regular line than is otherwise possible.

RETAINING WALLS

If it is found advisable to construct the garden on more than one level, much thought should be given to the selection of material and the design of the necessary steps and retaining walls.

How much more effective is a treatment of retaining walls (Fig. 121) than the slope, so generally adopted for each succeeding level! Such slopes are difficult to mow and, in a dry Summer, the turf burns out badly.

The use of stone as retaining walls between garden levels is not so generally adopted as it should be. The dry stone wall is especially worthy of greater use. The foundations of garden walls should always extend at least two feet six inches below grade and batter

Fig. 122.—The Hemlock forms an ideal hedge for the garden enclosure. The dark green color makes a pleasing background for the flowers.—See page 146

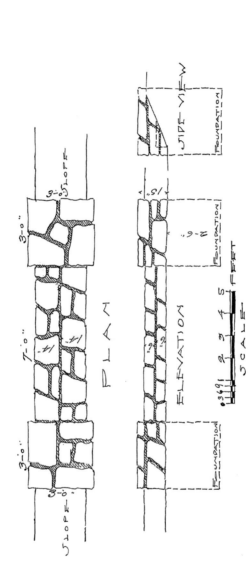

Fig. 123.—Plan for stone garden steps and cheek blocks. When there are a small number of risers it is possible to make the cheek blocks square.—See page 149

two inches to the foot. The thickness of retaining walls will depend on the height it is necessary to make them. As a general rule, a thickness at the base of one-half the height will be found satisfactory. A great deal depends, however, on the physical structure of the soil: a sandy, slippery soil will require a stronger wall than a hard, clayey soil, the latter being more self-retaining. Given a retaining wall with a northwest exposure, a scheme of wall planting is possible; pockets may be left in the wall and filled with soil for plants. Alyssum saxatile, Heuchera sanguineum, Sedums, Arabis albida, Aquilegias, Gypsophila, Valeriana, Santolina, and many other plants, are suitable for such a purpose.

GARDEN STEPS

Garden steps (Fig. 123) built of stone or brick require a greater breadth of treatment than is necessary for these features in connection with buildings. The risers should be close to six inches, and the tread at least fourteen inches in width.

Steps either approaching the garden, or within the enclosure, may be built with cheek blocks at the ends or with the ends built into the slope and planted with Ivy or Euonymus to cover the raw appearance. This is more pleasing than the harsh lines of the cheek blocks.

PIERS

All retaining boundary walls should terminate in piers and the corners and entrances (Fig. 118) of walls and hedges should be defined by similar features.

When the piers are built in a garden where a hedge is to be the enclosure, the piers should be from twenty-four to thirty inches wide; the hedge should be kept the same width and not allowed to become wider than the piers.

Piers at corners or entrances should be built the same height as the wall and the coping (Fig. 118) returned around the pier as a mark of accentuation. An additional stone placed on top of the coping, and set back six or seven inches from the edge, is very effective.

Where the entrance is to be featured by a gate or arch it is necessary to have the piers higher than the wall. Under such conditions it is more pleasing to have a ramp (Fig. 124) from the top of the wall to a point near the top of the pier. This is more pleasing than to have the pier standing high above the wall.

The same treatment should be applied at the intersection of two walls when, for reasons of grade, it is necessary to keep one below the other.

If the garden is on several levels and it is necessary to keep the cross walls flush with the grade a ramp (Fig. 125) should be used to tie the side and cross walls together gracefully.

WALKS AND BEDS

The interior arrangement of walks and beds must be practical and simple in outline, avoiding a complication of geometrical figures which are unrestful and difficult to keep up. Straight lines (Fig. 126) always give more character than curved ones and are much easier to maintain.

WALKS—WIDTH

The width of the paths will be regulated more or less by the area devoted to the garden, but they should always be as broad as

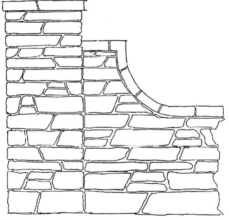

Fig. 124.—Ramp in wall to meet high pier at garden entrance.—See page 149

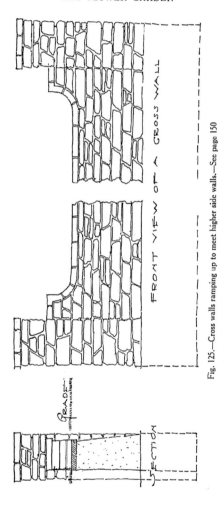

Fig. 125.—Cross walls ramping up to meet higher side walls.—See page 150

Fig. 126.—This shows the possibilities of making a picturesque garden on unpretentious lines. The beds are placed along the walks and the rectangular plats formed by the cross walks are left in turf. The Lombardy Poplars and conifers give a picturesque note to the scene, while the trees without, which are some distance from the enclosing hedge, form a pleasing setting.—See page 150

Fig. 127.—Turf walks are preferable for gardens. The greensward forms a canvas of pleasing color upon which to arrange the contrasting units of flowering plants.—See page 155

Fig. 128.—An effective use of brick for a garden walk, with bricks on edge for a border.—See page 155

the space will allow. In the smallest formal garden the minimum width should be four feet for the main paths, while the others may be as small as two and one-half feet.

WALKS—MATERIALS

Garden walks may be constructed of a variety of materials; among the most popular are gravel, brick, field stones, flagstone, tan bark and turf. The element of color is important and should be given careful consideration. For this reason the grayish tint of crushed stone is not pleasing; limestone is too glaring.

TURF WALKS

The turf path (Fig. 127) is the most attractive of all. It is pleasant to walk on, restful to the eye, and blends delightfully with the varying shades of color in the plantings. It makes a harmonious groundwork for floral effects desired without fear of discordant contrast.

BRICK WALKS

Bricks of rich, dark shades (Figs. 128 and 129) are very agreeable for garden walks. Occasional application of boiled linseed oil will darken the surface and give a more beautiful texture. The bricks should be laid in the basket (Fig. 50) or herring bone pattern (Fig. 52), with a neat border on end or edge.

RED GRAVEL

If red gravel is used it should be spread over a base of crushed stone at least four inches deep, and there should not be less than two inches of gravel, rolled and thoroughly compacted.

STEPPING STONES

The field stone or stepping stone walk (Fig. 53) is picturesque and gives an appearance of age to the garden. A single row of stones is much the best arrangement, as it leaves a greater portion of the walk in greensward.

FLAGSTONES

Flagstones laid with turf interstices are a change and give a satisfactory transition from the lawn to the utilitarian feature. The stones may be laid regularly or broken in irregular shapes and laid in broken range. If a mortar joint is used (Figs. 44 and 45) it should be finished flush with the stone surface.

SLATE

Slate slabs, laid the same as the flagstones, are very pleasing in color and are very serviceable. Slates may be had beautifully mottled with brown and gray.

TANBARK

Tanbark walks have fallen into disuse, most likely on account of the care and expense of upkeep. The color is good and the texture comfortable under foot. The sub-base for tanbark should be the same as for macadam, with an inch of the tanbark as a finish. A curb or border is necessary to keep the material within bounds.

BORDERS

When gravel, brick or tanbark is used in path construction it should be bordered with turf or Box (Fig. 129), or both. Turf borders should not be less than twelve inches wide and, where space permits, wider. If the turf border is too narrow the periodic edging reduces it to irregular widths. For this reason stone or brick on end or edge is often preferable.

GARDEN BEDS—WIDTH

Beds which may be reached from two sides can be six feet wide; those which can be worked from one side only should not be more than three feet wide.

The beds should never be placed next to a hedge, as the roots of the stronger growing hedge plants become very troublesome to the cultivated and enriched area. Under some conditions it is not possible to avoid having a bed next to the hedge; in such cases a three-inch concrete wall, two and one-half feet deep, constructed along the inside of the hedge, will help to force the hedge roots in the opposite direction.

PREPARING GARDEN BEDS

A successful garden will depend greatly on the preparation of the soil, care in planting and the upkeep. Garden beds should contain from eighteen inches to two feet of good friable soil. If it is not possible to supply all beds with this amount of good soil enriched with well rotted cow manure, the available top soil on the garden area should be stripped, the manure dug into the bottom soil

Fig. 129.—Brick garden walk, laid diagonally on edge and bordered with Box.—See pages 155, 156

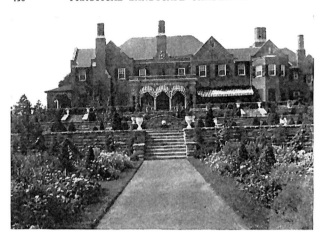

Figs. 130 and 131.—"The construction and setting of the garden are second in importance to the floral ensemble."   Contrast these two scenes !—See page 159

and the top soil replaced. If the bottom soil is heavy and does not afford good drainage, sufficient sand or coal ashes should be added in addition to the manure. A free circulation of air and abundant moisture are requisites of root growth; and soil preparation should be such that will make these readily available. Coal ashes worked into bottom soil will afford good drainage and, at the same time, supply moisture from the lower strata by capillary attraction.

HUMUS

Humus in the form of decayed vegetable matter from bogs or lakes should be used generously in preparing garden beds. This material is rich in plant foods and, worked well into the surface soil, lessens the tendency to puddle or bake.

FLORAL TREATMENT

The construction and setting of the garden, essential as these are to its success, are second in importance to the floral ensemble (Figs. 130 and 131). In the selection and arrangement of the flowers (Fig. 132) a great deal of liberty may be exercised and personal tastes indulged. The best planned and most enjoyable gardens are those which provide a sequence of bloom, starting with the Snowdrops and Crocuses in early Spring and continuing on through the Spring, Summer and Fall until the waning season is brightened by such old favorites as the Japanese Anemones and ushered out by the hardy Chrysanthemums.

An important subject to be considered in the arrangement of the flowers is that of balance. The height of the foliage and bloom on one side of the garden should have a corresponding unit on the other, not necessarily the same plant, but there should be some degree of similarity in outline and color.

Much has been written of color in the garden. I would lay stress on these few points. It is well to keep the purples and blues at some distance from the principal point of view; the lighter colors should be in the foreground. This will enhance the distance and give a pleasing graduation of color.

The question of mass should be given consideration. Most of the perennials have but a short season of bloom after which they are of little use. In selecting varieties for large clumps, those with a long blooming season should be chosen. Exceptions to this rule

Fig. 132.—Larkspurs in the garden. The selection and arrangement of the flowers should be the chief charm of the garden.—See pages 159, 162

Fig. 133.—"Bulbs should have a more intimate place in the garden than is customary. Not in straight rows but planted in clumps along the edges of the beds."—See page 162

are such plants as German and Japanese Irises. These plants have foliage of artistic excellence contrasting well with other features in the garden.

Very often large spaces occupied by plants of short blooming season may be brightened by the use of some Summer flowering bulbs, such as the Gladioli. Larkspurs (Fig. 132), Phlox, some of the Bellflowers, Chrysanthemums, and Japanese Anemones are good in masses.

BULBS

Bulbs should have a more intimate place in the garden than is customary (Fig. 133). Not in straight rows, but planted in clumps along the edges of the beds.

ANNUALS

Regardless of the care exercised in the selection and placing of the plants, the garden will not be altogether a success without the introduction of annuals (Fig. 134). Among the annuals are some of the most showy and useful plants that we have and they can be raised at a very small cost.

Annuals are familiar to all and it is only necessary to say that the dull spots and bare spaces in the garden may be brightened if a little forethought is given each Spring to the raising of some Pansies, Snapdragons, Asters, Larkspurs, Zinnias, and other easily transplanted kinds.

The time to sow annuals is in the months of April and May. The directions printed on the package as to the seeding, soil, watering and care should be followed closely.

For the time and expense required nothing will return so large a dividend in wealth of color and general satisfaction as the use of annuals.

HARDY SHRUBS

Hardy shrubs, too, have a place in the flower garden. Where the breadth is sufficient to allow unhampered development, these plants will give more character to the garden and afford a background for the flowers. Their use is appreciated in breaking up broad views and establishing vistas to distant and interesting points. The Deutzias, Philadelphus coronarius, Kerria japonica, Viburnums, Syringas, Spiræas and Buddleias are all good shrubs for garden use. Planted as specimens they should be well separated, always leaving ample space for the herbaceous plants between the individual shrubs. Oftentimes shrubs in the garden may be utilized to shade and protect some rather tender perennials or hardy bulbs.

EVERGREENS

Unless we would have the garden almost devoid of interest during the Winter months it is well to introduce some evergreens. These should be placed at regular intervals and always at the corners and ends of the beds, where they are bisected by walks (Fig. 135). If a large area is provided in the center of the garden for some such ornament as a sundial or bird bath, evergreens may be used here to good effect. The pyramidal conifers are the best suited for garden planting, and such varieties as pyramidal Box, Biotas, Arborvitæs and tall Junipers are recommended.

For general garden planting varieties having dark green foliage are most desirable. Junipers with light colored foliage, such as chinense and virginiana glauca, contrast poorly with the foliage of the flowers and against the gray stone of garden enclosures, when stone is used. The golden tipped kinds, too, should be omitted from the garden.

TREATMENT OF GARDENS CONSTRUCTED ON MORE THAN ONE LEVEL

When the garden is situated on two or three levels it is often very practicable to devote the first level to the Winter garden planted to evergreens with areas of turf; the second plateau to perennials; the third to Roses (Fig. 136). Where only two levels exist, combine the perennials and the Roses by placing the Roses around the outer edge and the herbaceous plants and annuals in the inner beds.

PLANTING AROUND GARDEN ENCLOSURES

The outside line of the garden enclosure on the lawn side should always be hidden with foliage. A mixed plantation of flowering shrubs, with a few pyramidal evergreens at the corners, is very effective. In the Southern States, where many of the broad-leaved evergreens are hardy, the English Laurels, Laurestinus and Carolina Cherry, should be more widely used in such plantings. The flowering shrubs outside the garden, lifting their heads above the garden enclosure, add a charm to the scene quite in tune with the

Fig. 134.—Annuals used as a border in a garden with turf walks, showing a good treatment of walks, beds and plants. The arrangement and growth are such that the outlines of the beds are lost in the general scene, the whole making a pleasing picture.—See page 162

Fig. 135.—Evergreens in the garden should be placed at regular intervals. These are well arranged at the corners and ends of beds where they are bisected by the walks.—See page 163

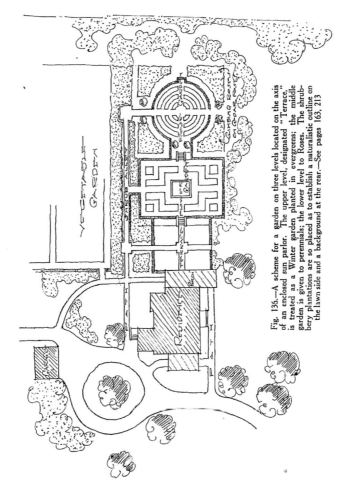

Fig. 135.—A scheme for a garden on three levels located on the axis of an enclosed sun parlor. The upper level, designated "Terrace," is treated as a Winter garden planted in evergreens; the middle garden is given to perennials; the lower level to Roses. The shrubbery plantations are so placed as to establish a naturalistic outline on the lawn side and a background at the rear.—See pages 163, 213

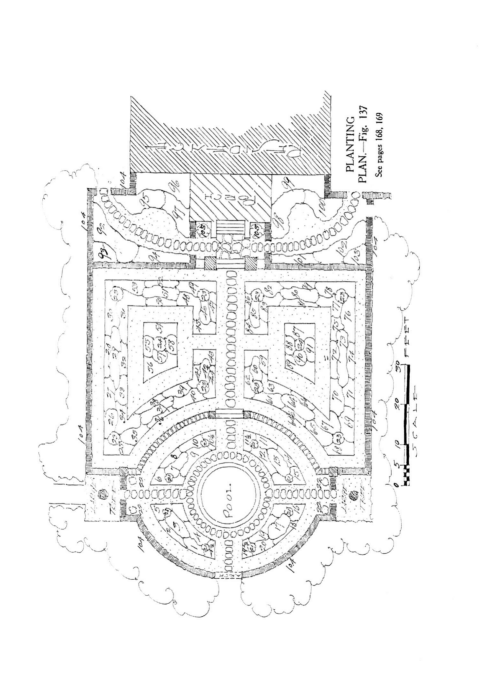

PLANTING
PLAN.—Fig. 137
See pages 168, 169

KEY TO PLANTING PLAN.—Fig. 137—See page 167

Fig. 137.—An interesting garden plan. A circular fountain and pool in the center of the elliptical garden on the lower level is the dominant feature.—See page 170

Key No.	Quan.	Variety	Common Name
1	9	Iris Kæmpferi, blue	Blue Japanese Flag
2	12	Phlox divaricata	Early Blue Phlox
3	7	Delphinium hybridum	Tall Larkspur
4	12	Stokesia cyanea	Stoke's Aster
4½	5	Funkia lancifolia	Plantain Lily
5	10	Iris pallida dalmatica	Lavender Flag
6	10	Iris candida	Flag
7	7	Anchusa, Dropmore var.	Alkanet
8	10	Veronica spicata	Speedwell
9	15	Platycodon Mariesi	Chinese Bellflower
10	7	Baptisia australis	False Indigo
10½	5	Funkia cærulea	Plantain Lily
11	7	Baptisia australis	False Indigo
11½	5	Funkia lancifolia	Plantain Lily
12	15	Stokesia cyanea	Stoke's Aster
13	7	Delphinium hybridum	Tall Larkspur
14	12	Phlox divaricata	Early Blue Phlox
15	10	Iris Yolande	Flag
16	10	Iris Thavista	Flag
17	7	Aconitum Napellus	Monkshood
18	10	Veronica spicata	Speedwell
19	15	Platycodon Mariesii	Chinese Bellflower
19½	5	Funkia cærulea	Plantain Lily
20	9	Iris Kæmpferi	Blue Japanese Flag
21	4	Taxus baccata fastigiata	Irish Yew
22	8	Taxus baccata fastigiata	Irish Yew
23	2	Cotoneaster Simonsii	Shining Rose Bo
24	8	Ilex aquifolium	English Holly
25	9	Iris Canary Bird	Yellow Flag
26	8	Hemerocallis flava	Day Lily
27	10	Pentstemon barbatus	Beard's Tongue
28	14	Arabis albida	Rock Cress
29	15	Phlox R. P. Struthers	Phlox
30	12	Aquilegia cærulea	Columbine
31	10	Pæonia grandiflora rubra	Red Peony
32	11	Iberis sempervirens	Candytuft
33	5	Gypsophila paniculata	Baby's Breath
34	7	Pæonia festiva maxima	White Peony
35	5	Digitalis purpurea	Foxglove
36	7	Funkia lancifolia	Plantain Lily
37	7	Chrysanthemum Sunshine	Chrysanthemum
38	9	Heuchera sanguinea	Alum Root
39	5	Delphinium chinense	Chinese Larkspur
40	7	Valeriana officinalis	Garden Heliotrope
41	5	Sedum spectabile	Showy Sedum
42	5	Iris Kæmpferi	Japanese Flag
43	7	Iris pallida dalmatica	Lavender Flag
44	7	Funkia japonica	Plantain Lily
45	7	Iris aurea	Yellow Flag
46	8	Iris Kæmpferi	Japanese Flag
47	5	Aquilegia cærulea	Columbine
48	9	Phlox l'Evenement	Pink Phlox

THE FLOWER GARDEN

Key No.	Quan.	Variety	Common Name
49	7	Rudbeckia Newmanni	Black-eyed Susan
50	7	Campanula persicifolia	Bellflower, Peach-leaved
51	7	Chrysanthemum Fairy Queen	Pink Chrysanthemum
52	7	Gaillardia compacta	Blanket Flower
53	8	Iris Kæmpferi	Japanese Flag
54	9	Aquilegia chrysantha	Yellow Columbine
55	5	Phlox Queen	White Phlox
56	10	Lupinus polyphyllus albus	Lupine
57	5	Lilium candidum	Madonna Lily
58	5	Phlox Slocum	Phlox
59	7	Iris Yolande	Purple Flag
60	5	Iris Kæmpferi	Japanese Flag
61	7	Valeriana coccinea	Scarlet Valerian
62	7	Funkia japonica	Plantain Lily
63	10	Statice Gmelini	Sea Lavender
64	7	Chrysanthemum Boston	Chrysanthemum
64½	7	Funkia lancifolia	Plantain Lily
65	9	Tritoma Pfitzeriana	Red Hot Poker Plant
66	7	Stokesia cyanea	Stoke's Aster
67	7	Pæonia Prince of Wales	Peony ⊙
68	9	Iris aurea	Yellow Flag
69	8	Coreopsis grandiflora	Tickseed
70	10	Scabiosa caucasica	Blue Bonnet
71	7	Gypsophila paniculata	Baby's Breath
72	9	Dianthus plumarius	Scotch Pink
73	15	Phlox Pantheon	Phlox
74	9	Campanula rotundifolia	Harebell
75	5	Delphinium chinense	Chinese Larkspur
76	14	Rudbeckia purpurea	Cone Flower
77	5	Pæonia Duke of Wellington	Peony
78	8	Iris Kæmpferi	Japanese Flag
79	10	Platycodon Mariesii	Chinese Bellflower
80	7	Chrysanthemum Klondike	Chrysanthemum
81	10	Geum coccineum	Avens
82	7	Artemisia lactiflora	
83	9	Phlox Van Hochberg	Phlox
84	7	Iris Mme. Chereau	Flag
85	8	Iris Kæmpferi	Japanese Flag
86	7	Aquilegia cærulea	Rocky Mountain Columbine
87	10	Lupinus Moerheimi	Lupine
88	5	Phlox Ingeberg	Hardy Phlox
89	9	Aquilegia Skinneri	Columbine
90	5	Lilium candidum	Madonna Lily
91	5	Phlox Thor	Hardy Phlox
92	9	Rhododendron roseum elegans	Pink Hybrid Rhododendron
93	3	Rhododendron Wilsoni	Dwarf Rhododendron
94	10	Rhododendron punctatum	Dwarf Rhododendron
95	7	Rhododendron caractacus	Red Rhododendron
96	7	Rhododendron purpurea elegans	Purple Rhododendron
97	5	Rhododendron Boule de Neige	Hybrid Rhododendron
98	5	Rhododendron Boule de Neige	Hybrid Rhododendron
99	7	Rhododendron purpurea elegans	Purple Rhododendron
100	7	Rhododendron caractacus	Red Rhododendron
101	10	Rhododendron punctatum	Dwarf Rhododendron
102	9	Rhododendron roseum elegans	Pink Rhododendron
103	3	Rhododendron Wilsoni	Dwarf Rhododendron
104	500	Ligustrum ovalifolium	California Privet

floral effects within, and the sinuous outline of the border plantation is in perfect harmony with the naturalistic aspect of the garden from without. At desirable viewpoints the planting should be low so that a glimpse may be had of the lawn, plantations or distant scenes.

Lilacs are particularly good for planting immediately outside the garden enclosure; also the Japanese Snowballs, the Rose of Sharon, and Deutzias. It is here that we may use the shrubs of upright character that produce their greatest wealth of bloom toward the top. Berried plants should also be considered in these plantations. The Wayfaring Tree (*Viburnum lantana*), Hercules' Club (*Aralia spinosa*), Photinia villosa, the Hawthorns, Burning Bush (*Euonymus*), Flowering Dogwood (*Cornus florida*), Bush Honeysuckle (*Lonicera*), and the deciduous Holly (*Ilex verticillata*), are all adaptable to such a purpose. Additional Winter color may be secured by planting the red and yellow twigged Dogwoods and, if the scope of the plantation admits, a few Red Birch.

The keynote of a successful garden setting is to so plant and arrange it that it will have the appearance of having existed before the garden was formed.

WATER IN THE GARDEN

A water feature (Fig. 137) is by far the most delightful note in the garden and gives added interest by reflecting the color of the flowers on its surface. It has the additional attribute of attracting the birds who come for their morning bath, thus adding a pleasing touch of life to the scene, usually augmented by a grateful carol of appreciation. More detailed notes on this subject will be found in the chapter on architectural features of the garden.

CHAPTER VIII

ARCHITECTURAL FEATURES OF THE GARDEN

The flower garden, even that of the tiniest dimensions, does not seem complete without some garden ornament, and in this day of great possibilities in this line, with the material procurable at but little expense, the desire is easy of fulfilment.

The architectural adornments of the garden cover many features: from the humble seat to the magnificent garden house.

The use of garden ornaments will depend greatly on their proper placing. The bird bath or fountain, placed in the center of a garden, on the axis of the paths, is appropriate and satisfying, even though it may be one of very simple design.

SUNDIALS

The sundial, upon which so many lines have been inscribed, both pleasant and harsh, is a garden ornament of many years' standing. The designs range from the simplest and most severe to the most elaborately ornate.

The sundial is usually treated as a central feature, or placed at the terminus of a walk, and is generally quite conspicuous as one enters the garden. It is, therefore, a pleasant relief at times to find it treated as an isolated feature and placed in some secluded nook where it conveys much more charm by coming upon it unexpectedly. If such a position is chosen care must be exercised in the plantings to avoid high growing plants which would interfere with the sun's rays on the dial.

The expertness with which cement is manipulated today has made it possible to produce substantial sundials at a moderate cost, and they may be had in many unique and diversified designs.

When setting the pedestal care should be taken to see that a substantial foundation is provided; this foundation may be constructed of brick, stone or concrete; if of brick or stone it should be laid in cement mortar.

If the sundial is placed where the turf will run up to the base the foundation should be built the neat width or diameter, as turf burns out readily in shallow soil over stone, brick or concrete.

In choosing a pedestal of artificial stone it is advisable to select one of simple outline and free from ornamentation, as the elements soon work havoc with the cement ornaments.

The sundial should always be elevated at least one foot above the surrounding level and the paved area should be wide enough to allow one to stand comfortably upon it when reading the dial.

BIRD BATHS

The bird bath (Fig. 138) is an attractive feature, worthy of much wider usage. It is not alone charming as an architectural feature, but has the additional merit of attracting the birds to the confines of the garden, enlivening the scene by the touch of life, color and song.

The bird font should be set in a conspicuous position where the little feathered visitors may be watched from some vantage point.

It is important to provide a firm foundation for the font and to furnish water direct through a galvanized wrought iron pipe connected with the general water supply. A good fountain spray may be secured by using an adjustable hose nozzle, which will provide a single column of water or a fine spray, whichever is desired.

The basin should always be placed on a fairly high pedestal as a protection against cats and other animals which prey upon the birds.

FOUNTAINS AND POOLS

The fountain (Fig. 139) is a garden feature greatly admired by all. The sound of falling water is ever a source of great delight. When the fountain has a surrounding pool the water should always be on the same level as the garden, or below that level. Instances are frequent where this rule is not observed and the water allowed to rise to a plane above the surrounding ground. The lack of repose in such a pool is very noticeable; such a situation is incorrect.

Pools or fountains (Fig. 140) are at their best when placed in the center of the garden or at the end of a vista down a garden walk or broad turf area.

DEPTH

Pools should never be less than twenty-two inches deep when it is desired to grow Water Lilies. Two feet or two feet six inches are even better depths.

CONSTRUCTION

Pool walls (Fig. 141) may be constructed of brick or concrete.

Brick walls should be one and one-half brick thick, coated on the inside with a Portland cement mortar in which some waterproofing should be incorporated. The bricks should be laid in a waterproofed cement mortar.

Concrete walls should be six inches thick, consisting of five inches of reinforced concrete and a one-inch finish coat. A waterproofing material should be incorporated both in the general mix and in the finish coat, or a damp-proofing and bonding paint applied to the rough surface before the finish coat is applied.

Pool bottoms will depend on the size of the pool and the character of the soil. They should have a base of cinders or crushed stone, to prevent heaving, on which should be laid a slab of five inches of waterproofed reinforced concrete with a finish coat of one inch. If concrete walls are to be built the reinforcing iron should be long enough to turn up.

POOL COPING

The coping may be of good hard brick laid on edge, or on what is called row-lock fashion; this is much to be preferred to the cut limestone or cement coping.

The gray sandstone (Fig. 140) to be had in the vicinity of Philadelphia is an excellent stone for this purpose, using either dressed or selected flat pieces, laid quarry face, uniform thickness, using one through cross stone alternately with two pieces showing a joint through the center.

The coping or curb should never stand more than four inches above the surrounding grade; the closer the coping level is to the garden grade the more pleasing will be the appearance.

A sod edge extending to the pool has a softness and a natural appearance which have much to commend it. When a sod edge is desired the side walls of the pool should be beveled back to give as much depth as possible to the soil around the edge for the proper support of the turf. Under some conditions boulders around the margin are pleasing, particularly when the position is somewhat shaded, and ferns and other shade enduring plants may be planted between the boulders.

THE BIRD BATH

Fig. 138.—"The bird bath attracts the birds to the confines of the garden, enlivening the scene by the touch of life, color and song."—See page 172

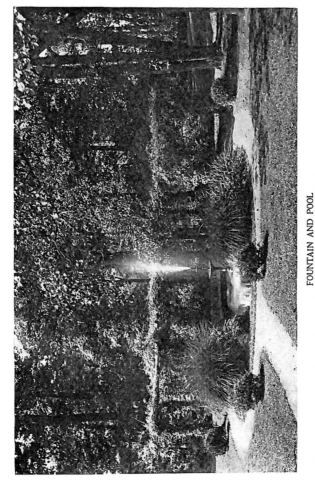

FOUNTAIN AND POOL

Fig. 139.—The rustic pergola in the background of the garden fountain is an added allurement to a quiet retreat.—See page 172

GARDEN POOL WITH WATER LILIES

Fig. 140.—" Pools are at their best when placed in the center of the garden or at the end of a vista down a garden walk or broad turf area."—See pages 172, 173, 179

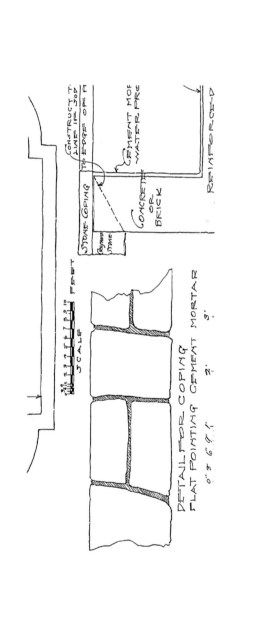

CONSTRUCT T
AND IN JOP
EDGE OF R

STONE COPING

CONSTRUCT T
TO EDGE OF R

POINTED
STONE

CEMENT MOF
WATER PRE

CONCRETE
OR
BRICK

REINFORCED

SCALE

FEET

3 2 1 0 1 2 3 4 5 6 7 8 9 10

DETAIL FOR COPING
FLAT POINTING CEMENT MORTAR

0'   3"   6"   9"   1'   2'   3'

WATER SUPPLY AND DRAINAGE

The pool should be connected with the general water supply, if practicable, and a drain provided (Fig. 141) so that the pool may easily be emptied, cleaned and refilled. The most economical and practical method to arrange for the overflow and drainage is to have a standpipe with a ground beveled end to fit in a socket set at the low point of the pool. The size of the pipe will depend on the amount of water, but, for ordinary purposes, a one and one-half inch pipe is sufficient to carry off the overflow. To drain the pool it is only necessary to remove the standpipe.

Another method of providing for the overflow and drainage is to have a concealed standpipe (Fig. 142) built into the end wall of the pool. When the water rises to the top of the standpipe at A, it overflows. To drain, the standpipe is removed through a concealed opening at B.

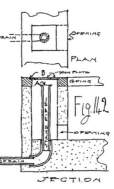

Fig. 142.—Concealed standpipe for garden pool overflow and drainage.

Where the drain is controlled by a valve, the valve should be set in a small box with an iron cover set flush with the grade.

From a point immediately outside the walls of the pool the water may be carried off by a three-inch terra cotta pipe.

The appearance of the pool will be greatly improved by placing an inch of clean pebbles over the bottom.

GARDEN POOLS WITH FOUNTAIN HEADS

Oftentimes garden pools are placed at the ends of the gardens fed from a fountain head placed in a vertical wall.

The construction of such pools should be similar to that already outlined.

The vertical wall should rise above the wall enclosing the garden to emphasize the feature.

Fountains and pools so located should be provided with a good background, preferably evergreens of a dark shade; the Red Cedar and similar types are admirable for the purpose.

PLANTING NEAR GARDEN POOLS

The planting near garden pools should include some bright colored flowering plants in positions where they will reflect all the glory of their color on the surface of the water, for the pool is a delightful outdoor mirror, reflecting all its environment with a softness that is most charming.

PLANTS IN THE POOL

The garden pool is not complete, nor affording one of its greatest pleasures, if it does not support some Water Lilies (Fig. 140).

In tightly built pools it is necessary to plant the Lilies in tubs. A very economical and satisfactory tub may be provided by cutting in two an old vinegar or liquor barrel.

The soil for the proper support of the Lilies should consist of a good loam well enriched with decomposed cow manure, equal to one-fifth of the entire bulk. On top of this place two inches of bar sand. The tubs should be set to a depth that will allow about six inches of water over the soil.

THE PLANTS

For the average garden pool a selection from the many varieties obtainable of hardy and tender Nymphæas will be found most satisfactory.

These may be planted just as they start into growth, usually about May 1 in the vicinity of Philadelphia; at that time all danger of frost is over and even the tender kinds may be safely set out.

Only sufficient fresh water need be supplied to the pool to provide for that lost through evaporation.

The Nelumbiums are very handsome, of easy culture and well suited to large pools. Other good aquatic plants are the Water Hyacinth, Water Snowflake, Papyrus or Umbrella Plant.

The hardy varieties may be left in the pool all Winter; but they require a protection of leaves, with evergreen boughs or boards over them to keep the leaves in place.

FISH

It is well to stock garden pools with goldfish to destroy mosquito larvæ, and to add the requisite touch of life and color.

SWIMMING POOLS

The loss of so many of the old-time swimming holes has developed a demand for the artificial swimming pool.

Fig. 143.—Swimming pool within the garden area. Gray sandstone coping to match the walls and steps

Such pools may often be placed within the garden area (Fig. 143).

The construction should be the same as that outlined for smaller pools, care being taken to waterproof the walls, not only from the standpoint of keeping the water within the pool, but to keep the moisture from outside from seeping through and discoloring the walls. The swimming pool may be incorporated in the flower garden as a wading pool or made sufficiently deep at one end to allow of diving, running from two to three feet deep at one end to from seven to eight feet deep at the other.

Swimming pools should be provided with a ladder to assist in leaving the pool at the deep end. A removable ladder is best for a combination garden and swimming pool. Rings should be supplied at intervals along the edge of the pool and a rope run through, so that bathers may grasp same for support when required.

WATER SUPPLY

Should the water supply come from a spring or stream on the premises it will be necessary to have a valve or plug to shut off the supply at the intake. When using water from a stream it is advisable to have a forebay set at one side and the pipe run from that to the pool. The forebay or well is built along the stream to prevent leaves, sand and debris from getting into the pipe. This is essential, regardlesss as to what method is adopted for conveying the water to the pool, either by gravity, ram, gas engine, electric pump or gasoline engine.

As swimming pools must be emptied frequently in order to cleanse them, a small electric pump may be introduced, where the power is at hand, and the water from the pool connected to the garden pipe line and so used for watering, thus conserving the general supply.

GARDEN SEATS

The value of the seat as a garden feature has long been recognized. A seat affords a comfortable and delightful resting place to those who would walk or work within the garden.

Seats should be placed on the axis of walks, in niches formed by planting, or in the enclosing garden wall (Fig. 144) or hedge, and roofed over if only in the most fragile way.

Where practicable, seats should be placed where they will command a good view of the garden (Fig. 145) or of some portion of the garden or its surroundings.

A novel seat (Fig. 146) is sometimes built on the axis of intersecting walks, consisting of two walls seven feet high, built in the shape of a cross, with the seats placed in each corner formed by the walls. With such a resting place one may always select a retreat sheltered from sun or wind, as desired, regardless of time of day or the quarter in which the wind happens to be.

For greatest comfort wooden seats are best. They may be had in great variety and to suit any taste or need.

Stone or artificial stone seats are more ornamental, but for real use are not as practical as those of wood. Stone seats should have a stone or concrete foundation, otherwise they will soon get out of level.

When purchasing artificial stone seats it is advisable to select those of simple design rather than those overlaid with ornament.

GARDEN HOUSES

The location and placing of garden houses and pergolas should always be considered when planning the garden and not as an after consideration.

Fig. 144.—WELL PLACED GARDEN SEAT WITH COVERING
See page 181

Fig. 145.—Garden seat commanding a good view of the garden.—See page 181

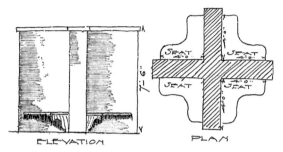

ELEVATION PLAN

Fig. 146.—A unique design for a sheltered garden seat to be placed on the axis of walks or in an isolated position commanding a pleasing vista. It is always possible to find a section sheltered from sun or wind.—See page 181

Although space is not usually available in a small garden for a garden or tea house, yet quite often a space can be found sufficient to make a little break outside the line; here it may be set in a niche, thus providing ease of access and possibly greater seclusion.

It is essential that such features be placed on the most dominant axis of the garden, as a terminal feature, or at one corner with a balancing feature in the opposite corner. In this location a covered house is more desirable and affords more protection. In open topped houses of pergola construction twigs and leaves are constantly falling from the overhanging vines so that, where it is desired to serve tea occasionally in the garden house, the closed top construction is preferable.

If the garden adjoins the residence the garden house should be built to conform with the architecture of the house; if isolated from the house the design may be one that will suit the individual taste and requirement (Figs. 147 and 147A). The rustic house, built of Red Cedar, lends itself to the greatest diversity.

Garden houses with but one open side should have a southern exposure, pre-eminently when there is a pretty outlook in that direction. Such a house will be found a delightful retreat in Autumn, where one may be sheltered from the cold winds and enjoy the view under most delightful conditions.

The floor of the garden house should be of enduring material,

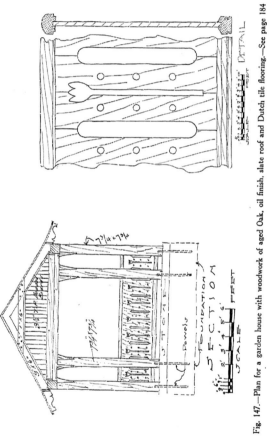

Fig. 147.—Plan for a garden house with woodwork of aged Oak, oil finish, slate roof and Dutch tile flooring.—See page 184

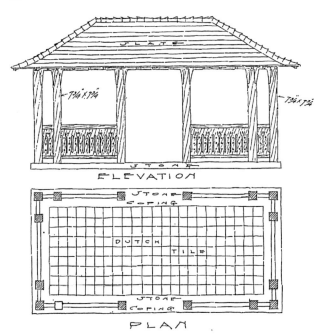

Plan and elevation for Fig. 147.—See pages 184, 185

such as flagstone, slate, brick, or tile; and, for permanency of construction, should be set on a concrete base four inches deep with a sub-base of stone or cinders. An inch of bar sand should be placed over the concrete as a cushion.

The old Dutch tile size, eight inches by eight inches by two inches, with a brick texture, makes a very satisfactory floor with a border of brick on the outside.

Garden houses should be set close to the ground and should not be more than twelve inches above the garden grade. A six-inch elevation, requiring a single step, is most hospitable in appearance.

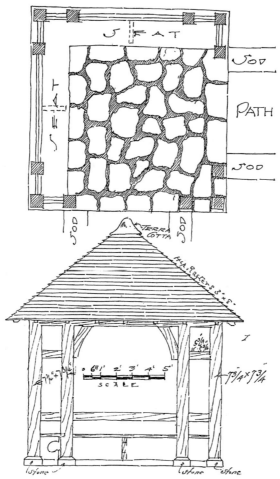

SEAT

SOD

PATH

SOD

SEAT

SOD   SOD
        TERRA
        COTTA

HIP RAFTERS 3×5″

7¾″×7¾″

0 6″1′ 2′ 3′ 4′ 5′
        SCALE

stone   stone   stone

147A.—Plan for a garden house, shingle or tile roof. Woodwork of aged Oak, oil
finish and flooring of flat stones.—See page 184

PERGOLAS

Garden houses of closed top construction are preferable to those of the pergola style within the garden. Pergolas used in the garden should be treated as terminal features (Fig. 148) or as covering walks leading to substantial terminals. Then the lights and shadows from the overhead construction (Fig. 149), with its covering of Roses and vines,, are very delightful.

Pergolas may be of wood, brick, stone or concrete construction, depending largely on the style of the garden enclosures, architecture of the house, and the design and general surroundings of the garden.

Pergolas built of wood may be of a rustic nature, using wood with the bark on, or constructed of planed wood, stained or painted.

For pergolas of a rustic nature Red Cedar is the best material to use. For those constructed with planed wood, White Pine or Cypress are best. The high cost of White Pine makes it almost prohibitive. California Red Wood and Douglas Spruce are suitable for this purpose. The cost of these latter two is more moderate than that of either Cypress or Pine.

If the columns are of wood they should be set in concrete (Fig. 150), first coating the wood that is imbedded in the concrete with a tar paint. If the posts are set in the ground, that part in the earth should always be coated with tar.

If rustic posts are used the bark should be stripped from their lower portions before placing them in the ground.

When setting posts in concrete, allow the concrete to come a little above grade (Fig. 150) with the top beveled so that the water can not seep down between it and the post.

Treat logs with kerosene, to preserve the bark and protect it against the ravages of borers, which tunnel under the bark and soon loosen it.

Pieces selected for the uprights should not be less than eight inches at the base, preferably twelve. Clearance space under the cross pieces should not be less than eight feet and the breadth from center to center of posts for this height, assuming a twelve-inch column, should be eight feet two inches, making the clearance between posts seven feet two inches, just ten inches less than the height.

Always avoid making the width greater than the height; for good proportion the reverse is always better.

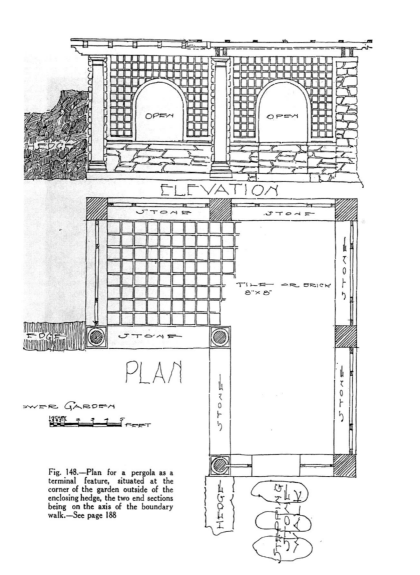

ELEVATION

PLAN

Fig. 148.—Plan for a pergola as a terminal feature, situated at the corner of the garden outside of the enclosing hedge, the two end sections being on the axis of the boundary walk.—See page 188

Fig. 149.—The lights and shadows from the overhead construction of the pergola, with its covering of Roses and vines, is delightful.—See page 188

If turned columns are used their height should be eight or nine times the diameter and the lintels should be of two three-inch by ten-inch pieces, notched over the cap. The rafters (Fig. 151) should be three inches by eight inches, notched over the lintels. For the better support of vines, additional pieces should be placed on top of the rafters, running at right angles to the same. These pieces may be one and one-eighth inches by two and three-quarter inches; or of shingling lath, planed down, which reduces them to about three-quarters of an inch by two and three-eighths inches. The rafters (Figs. 151-153) should have a projection of from eighteen inches to thirty inches and should be cut to a good bold outline.

The caps should always be covered with light sheet lead (Fig. 151) neatly tacked around the edge.

When stone is used for the support of the superstructure the columns or piers should not be less than twenty-two inches, and these should stand on a foundation twenty-eight inches square, which will allow of a three-inch projection all the way around.

The stones should be laid up in cement mortar and, where pointed, the pointing should conform to the pointing of the house, if the pergola is adjacent thereto. An effective method of laying up the stone work is to rake out the mortar joints to a depth of two to three inches; this will give a deep shadow and form a friendly supporting ledge for the vines.

Cap stones should be of the same stone as that used in the piers, flat and hammer dressed, without projection, and set flush with the stone work below. It

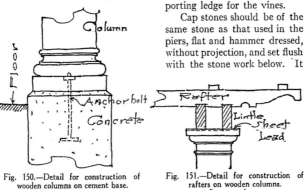

Fig. 150.—Detail for construction of wooden columns on cement base. See page 188

Fig. 151.—Detail for construction of rafters on wooden columns. See note above

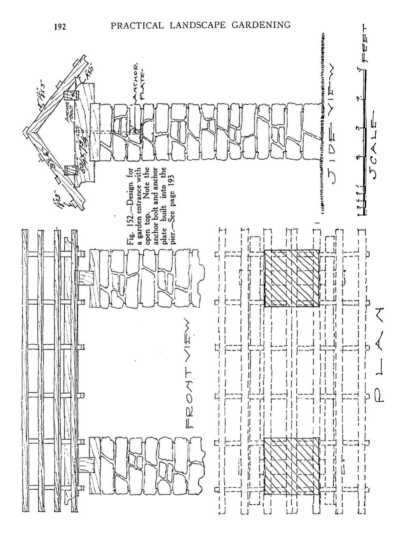

Fig. 152.—Design for a garden entrance with open top. Note the anchor bolt and anchor plate built into the pier.—See page 193

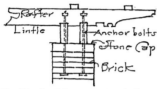

Fig. 153.—Detail for construction of rafters on brick piers. Note the stone cap. See also page 191

is not necessary that the cap be all one piece; when constructed of two or more pieces the joints should be pointed.

It is essential to build anchor bolts in the top of the columns (Fig. 152) to secure the lintels. These bolts should have a four-inch flat iron plate on the bottom to prevent the bolt from being pulled out of place when tightening the nut at the top.

Piers or columns constructed of brick should be of the dark shades; Harvard, Sayre and Fisher, or tapestry brick, are all suitable kinds. They may be laid up with either a broad mortar joint or reveal joints, raking out the mortar for a depth of two to three inches. Brick piers are improved by having a base and cap (Fig. 153) either of cut stone or of brick laid on end with a quarter-inch projection at the bottom and edgewise, set flush with the sides of the piers at the top.

There are times when light brick must be used to conform with the house; but light bricks are anemic looking for pergolas and should be used only when unavoidable.

Stucco columns (Fig. 154) may be built on tile, as it is substantial and economical. Stucco piers should be built on a foundation of stone or concrete projecting beyond the line of the tile. Twelve-inch tile is about the minimum size to use, as it is difficult to hold a smaller size plumb when building.

FLOORS

Pergola floors should be built with a view to permanency. The foundation should consist of eight or twelve inches of clean cinders wet and thoroughly compacted, or of equal depth of crushed stone on which should be laid a concrete slab four inches thick, composed of one part Portland cement to two of sharp sand and five of crushed one and one-half inch stone, thoroughly tamped. On this place a cushion of one-inch bar sand. Such a foundation should be provided for brick, slate, cement or stone paving. If concrete is not used in the foundations the cinders are best with the sand cushion placed directly on top of them. All paving should have a slight fall; an eighth or a quarter of an inch to the foot is sufficient. This will prevent surface water from collecting.

If brick, stone or slate is used for paving the joints should be pointed with a cement mortar to prevent grass and weeds growing in the interstices. It is seldom practical to successfully grow turf under pergolas, as the shade from the overhanging vines becomes too dense. On open terraces such a treatment is satisfactory and picturesque.

The cement finished floor is the least desirable of all. It has a harsh, mechanical finish which does not fit in with soft, responsive surroundings of the garden. If cement is used much of the glare may be reduced and the texture improved by tinting it. Lamp black and the red mortar stains are used for the purpose. They should be applied in the finish coat, and that rather sparingly, or the efficiency of the cement will be much impaired. Cement paving should have expansion joints cut at intervals to prevent cracking. A cement surface will have a better appearance if it is cut up into small rectangular blocks, either square or oblong in form.

The color of the timber superstructure will be largely influenced by that of the house; when adjacent to the house the color adopted should conform to the residence.

White may always be used with safety and will intensify the shades of green leafage by contrast. There are various shades of brown obtainable, from the tint resulting from the use of creosote "oil grade one" to the almost black shade of Van Dyke brown. These latter colors are especially attractve in combination with the brick or stone substructure.

COLOR OF WOODEN GARDEN FEATURES

The color of wooden garden features is a subject well worth considerable thought. White paint is used more frequently than any other and, although pleasing to the eye when the foliage is on the plants, it is most glaring and cold looking in the Winter season. Shades of green are good but do not afford sufficient contrast. On the whole, shades of brown and weathered oak tints will give the greatest satisfaction.

Fig. 154.—Stucco columns with rustic superstructure.—See page 193

Fig. 155.—An attractive hardy border.—See page 197

CHAPTER IX

HARDY BORDERS AND ROSE GARDENS

PERENNIAL BORDERS

Of the many ways in which the cultivation of flowers is undertaken none is so popular as the "mixed" or "hardy" border (Fig. 155). Such borders are seen on nearly every property and occupy different and varied positions. They may be planted in front of shrubbery belts (Fig. 156), in the kitchen garden (Fig. 159), along sides of walks (Fig. 165), and against walls and buildings (Fig. 157).

LOCATION OF HARDY BORDERS

It is to be regretted that hardy borders are usually placed to the rear of the house. Although some perennials do have a short season of bloom, and others are not provided with pleasing foliage, even with these deficiencies, if the selection of plants be carefully made, borders may be so planted that they will be attractive all through the season. On small places particularly, the flowers should be in the front, much as they are in the cottage gardens of England, where borders along walks and fences are so attractively treated. In these plantings it is obvious that the floral arrangement is given preference to the outline of the beds and this is as it should be. Irregular beds of meaningless outline should be avoided and the simplest forms adopted.

AVOID BORDERS NEXT TO A HEDGE

Perennial borders should never be planted against a hedge; it is preferable to leave about two or three feet between the hedge and the bed. Many plantings are ruined after the first year or two by the roots of hedge plants which grow apace in the enriched soil of the flower borders.

TURF EDGE FOR BEDS

When borders are placed along walks it is advisable to leave at least eighteen inches of turf (Fig. 166) between the bed and the walk. It is difficult to mow and trim a narrower strip.

BORDERS ALONG A FENCE

A very satisfactory arrangement of beds along a fence (Fig. 158) is to have a narrow bed, say two feet wide, for the taller growing varieties right against the fence, then a turf strip, two and one-half or three feet between this and a larger bed on the lawn side. This will afford a charming vista and give more variety to the scene.

BORDERS IN THE VEGETABLE GARDEN

The vegetable garden (Fig. 159) may be much improved by the introduction of perennial borders along the walks which bisect it and also along the outer walks. It is not necessary to sacrifice, to any great extent, the utilitarian side of the garden for this esthetic feature, as the beds may be made quite narrow (Fig. 160). From four to five feet is a desirable width and will afford an area suscepti-ble of very pleasing treatment. It is well to give character to bor-ders of this kind by planting tall flowering shrubs at the corners formed by the intersection of the walks and at the outside corners.

WIDTH OF BORDERS

The width of the borders will vary somewhat according to location. In the open, where it is practical to reach beds from both sides, they may be made six feet wide. In positions where they can only be reached from one side the width should not exceed four feet; three feet is preferable.

PREPARATION OF BEDS

In itself the word " hardy " is suggestive that permanency should be the first consideration in the planting of such a border, so that with but simple care the plants will continue for years. It is essen-tial, therefore, that thorough preparation of the soil be made before planting. Two feet of good soil, well enriched with plant food, should be provided for borders. Well rotted manure, finely ground bone and well pulverized sheep manure, in equal parts by weight, are good fertilizers for perennials.

TIME TO PLANT

Very early Spring, just as the plants are starting into growth, is the most favorable season for planting the majority of perennials. Do not plant in wet soil; it is better to wait until the ground is fairly dry. In some localities the Spring season is very short and uncertain; this may call for planting to be done in the Fall. Plants

Fig. 156.—Hardy Phlox in a border planting in front of shrubbery.—See page 197

Fig. 157.—Hardy Chrysanthemums in a border along a wall.—See page 197

Fig. 158.—Plan for perennial borders along a fence and at the corner of a lawn. In the bed along the fence plant high growing perennials and the lower growing kinds in the outer bed. —See page 198

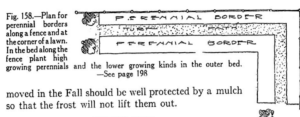

moved in the Fall should be well protected by a mulch so that the frost will not lift them out.

SUMMER CARE

Summer care of perennials will consist principally of frequent cultivation so as to allow a full circulation of air and to keep down the weeds. Tall growing plants should be staked so that the borders will present a neat appearance. Staking should be done as the plants grow, and not at the last moment when the weight of foliage and flowers has made it impossible to give proper support.

To get the best result with hardy borders they should be gone over every year so that some of the very rampant plants, such as Coreopsis, can be kept in check. It is usually the late blooming varieties which need more frequent division and transplanting. Spring blooming plants flower mostly from root crowns or buds perfected the preceding year; the Fall blooming plants from the numerous new stems produced during the growing season. Some of the strong growing Fall bloomers lose the original crown every year, leaving many side shoots which spread rapidly through the borders. Plants of this type should be dug up and replanted, setting back just a few of the strongest roots. This will insure larger and better blossoms and more kindly consideration of neighboring plants.

ARRANGEMENT OF PLANTS IN HARDY BORDERS

The arrangement of plants in the hardy border (Fig. 161) should be with a view to color effect and sequence of bloom. The beds should be interesting from early Spring to late Fall. The most difficult plants to handle successfully with a view to good color effect are those with magenta and mauve shades. It is safe to separate these from conflicting shades with white and pale yellow. The white must be used sparingly, however, as it is the most conspicuous color in the combination. The scarlet shades are the high lights in the garden and we cannot place magentas or blues too close to the scarlets with satisfactory results. It is better to pass from orange and yellow to blue.

Fig. 159.—The appearance of the vegetable garden may be improved by the introduction of perennial borders along the outer walks.—See pages 197, 198

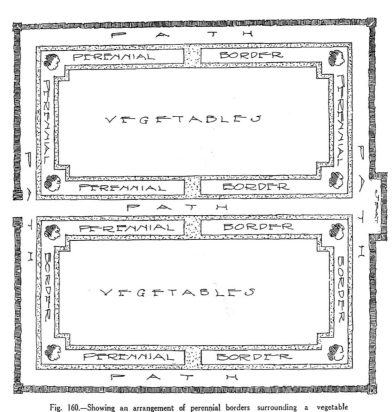

Fig. 160.—Showing an arrangement of perennial borders surrounding a vegetable garden.—See page 198

Fig. 161.—An attractively planted border showing what a pleasing effect may be produced with a small variety of plants. The Delphiniums give height and dignity to the scene, and the Iris and Funkias an agreeable contrast of foliage.—See page 200

To get a good color scheme and sequence of bloom it is well to make a plan of the beds first and figure out the spaces and the quantities, such as has been done on the plans illustrated. To facilitate this work a list of plants to be used, arranged according to season of bloom, height and color, will be of great help.

BORDER BEDS SHOULD NOT BE GRADUATED EVENLY AS TO HEIGHT

It is a mistake to plant all the rear row with tall plants, the middle rows with medium growing ones, and the border with low varieties. More consideration should be given to the profile or, as the artist would say, the "sky line." To obtain the most pleasing effects with perennials plant so that the taller varieties (Fig. 162) will stand out boldly and not be held up on both sides by some other tall kind. Set off the Larkspurs (Fig. 162), Hollyhocks (Fig. 163), or Foxgloves by some lower growing kind next to them, and show the medium growing varieties to better advantage by introducing tall kinds for contrast.

BACKGROUND FOR BORDERS

Where space permits of long borders of good width the question of a suitable background (Fig. 164) should not be entirely overlooked. Good supporting growth adds greatly to the charm and attractiveness of perennial plantings. For this reason it is well to introduce shrubs or evergreens at regular intervals in borders along walks. These will strengthen the planting and add to the character.

ROSE CHAINS IN PERENNIAL BORDERS

Another pleasing addition to the perennial border is the introduction of cedar posts at intervals of from ten to twelve feet, through which, at a point about ten inches from the top of the post, a chain of one and one-half inch links should be run. Plant a climbing Rose at each post, to form a pillar of green, and train the leaders along the chain to form a festoon.

ARCHES OVER WALKS

Rose arches (Fig. 165) are pleasing to tie together border beds along walks and increase the apparent distance. These should not be planted too closely together; fifteen to twenty feet apart is the most satisfactory distance.

PLANTING IN CLUMPS

It is not advisable to dot single plants of favorite varieties all through the borders. Rather, have some good clumps (Fig. 166)

at one, two, or several places in the bed. Too much stress cannot
be laid on this point. Keep varieties together; do not scatter them
too much. The effect is better; it helps greatly in the care of the
beds, and allows of keeping in much closer touch with individuals.
The size of the clumps will depend greatly on the area of the borders
and the location. Care should be taken not to plant large clumps
of varieties which have a very limited blooming season, such as the
Oriental Poppy, or kinds with poor foliage, such as Anthemis tinc-
toria. Frequent small clumps of such kinds are better with Gladioli
planted among them for later bloom.

BULBS AND TUBERS

Greater use should be made of bulbs and tubers in the hardy
borders. They are inexpensive and should otherwise be considered
from the standpoint of ease of culture, color, and succession of
bloom. It is possible, by a careful selection, to secure a sequence of
bloom lasting through the entire season.

Bulbs and tubers may be generally divided into two classes;
those known as hardy bulbs, such as Daffodils and Crocuses, which
may be allowed to remain in the border from season to season; and
tender bulbs, such as Gladioli and Dahlias, which must be lifted and
wintered under cover. These classes may again be divided into
Spring, Summer and Fall blooming kinds.

SPRING BULBS

Of the Spring kinds nearly all are suitable for garden culture.
Among the first to bloom, usually as early as February, we have
Winter Aconite (*Eranthis hyemalis*), Snowdrops and Crocuses,
followed by Daffodils, early and late Tulips and Hyacinths.

The late blooming Tulips, such as the Darwins, Cottage and
Parrot types, deserve more general recognition in our garden beds.
They afford magnificent coloring and have good long stems, making
them suitable for use as cut flowers.

SUMMER FLOWERING BULBS

Of the Summer flowering bulbs and tubers the Gladiolus and
Dahlia are the best known.

Gladioli may be had in very choice colors and are unexcelled for
planting among Peonies and other herbaceous plants with heavy
foliage and but a very short blooming season. Gladioli may be

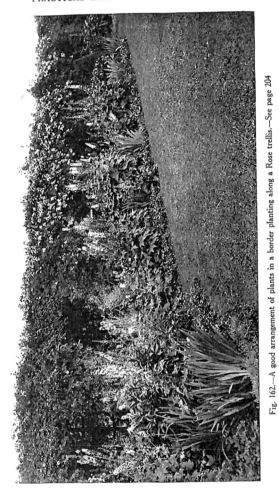

Fig. 162.—A good arrangement of plants in a border planting along a Rose trellis.—See page 204

Fig. 163.—Hollyhocks in a border planting.—See page 204

Fig. 164.—This early flowering border of Iris, Peonies, Foxgloves and English Daisies illustrates the advantages of a background. The Funkia cordifolia, as a center feature at the corner, is well placed.—See page 204

Fig. 165.—This picturesque rear yard is most artistically planted. The fence line is bordered with high growing perennials and a turf walk, two feet wide, divides it from a larger border on the lawn. The small border along the walk to the garage is planted with Roses and Rose arches tie the beds together and apparently increase the distance.—See pages 197, 204

planted weekly from May to July, and will afford a succession of bloom through the Summer.

Dahlias given but ordinary treatment in the garden will repay one with a wealth of bloom in the late Summer and Fall months. Varieties may be had in many forms and colors to suit the individual taste. Plant young plants in preference to tubers and give them an open, sunny position. The plants should be kept upright and tidy by the use of supports.

Tuberous rooted Begonias may be introduced into the shaded portions of the garden and will afford a variety of gay colors in large and beautiful flowers. They are more effective when planted together in a bed rather than scattered through the garden. Better treatment can be afforded them in this way as they need a light but rich soil for the best results. The tubers should be started indoors to ensure early bloom.

The Summer Hyacinth (*Hyacinthus candicans*) is a splendid Summer flowering bulb to scatter through the borders in clumps of five or more. The bell-shaped flowers appear on long stems, three to five feet high; there are as many as thirty flowers on a stem.

Many of the Lilies are hardy and may be successfully introduced into the borders. Groups of L. auratum (the gold-banded Lily of Japan); L. elegans, a lovely, upright, orange-colored type; L. speciosum, a Japanese variety, and L. tigrinum, the old-fashioned Tiger Lily, are the best for border use.

The Tuberose is an old-fashioned favorite, rather stiff, it is true, but very fragrant and beautiful. By careful management, starting to plant as soon as the conditions are favorable in the Spring and continuing until July, a succession of bloom may be had all Summer.

The Eremurus, or Giant Asphodel, might well be classed among Summer flowering bulbs, as it has a stout, fleshy root with a central crown from which the rootlets radiate. Well drained land and plenty of plant food are requisites. The flowers come on tall stalks sometimes eight to ten feet high. The flowers form on the upper part of the stalk and continue to form as the stem lengthens. Eremurus needs considerable room in the border, so should only be used where extensive space is to be had. It should be set in the Autumn, planted at least six inches deep.

AUTUMN BULBS

Of the Autumn flowering bulbs, Colchicum autumnale, the Meadow Saffron or Autumn Crocus, is perhaps best known. The flowers very much resemble Crocuses. The bulbs should be planted in July and August, in clumps, not too set looking, in the front of the borders. They may be had in white, lilac and blue.

The Red Hot Poker plant, or Tritoma, may be classed among the Autumn flowering bulbous plants worthy of a place in all hardy borders. The orange, coral red and yellow flowers are very striking. Some of the newer kinds have early, free, and continuous blooming qualities, and succeed in an ordinary garden soil. Tritomas are not altogether hardy in some locations and, for safety, should be lifted in the Fall and wintered under cover, buried in sand in a cool cellar or shed.

The Montbretia is a hardy bulbous plant that should be in every flower border. The flowers are brightly colored, mostly orange red, and on stems from two to three feet high. They should be planted in an open, sunny position. Bulbs may be set in the Autumn or very early Spring.

ANNUALS IN THE BORDERS

Very often the effect of perennial beds is marred by allowing too much bare soil to show, particularly along the edges. This may be overcome by planting cover plants, or in the new border by planting an assortment of annuals. As hardy cover plants the Candytuft, Creeping Phlox, early blue Phlox, Plumbago, Rock Cress, and many similar varieties, are splendid. Of the annuals many kinds are suitable for border planting; among the best are Sweet Sultan, Silene, Coreopsis, Larkspur, Balsam, Zinnia, Dianthus, Eschscholtzia, Aster, Godetia, Clarkia, Snapdragon, Calendula and Poppy. Annuals are very easily grown. If wanted early, the seeds should be started indoors in flats. Many kinds may be quickly and easily grown by sowing in the open ground when danger of frost is over.

Really, the material for hardy beds is inexhaustible and a selection may be made for a constant succession of bloom through the entire season. If they are planned carefully, remembering that it is the contents of the beds and not the outline that is attractive, and with the idea of permanency before us, such borders will continue for years with but little care.

ROSE GARDENS

Every one knows how satisfactory the Rose is for outdoor decoration and for cutting, but it does not receive all the considera-

Fig. 166.—Better effects may be secured in hardy border through planting in clumps rather than scattering single plants all through the border. Note turf edge between walk and bed.—See pages 197, 204

tion it deserves in our gardens. No garden is complete without some of this queen among flowers.

ROSE GARDEN DESIGNS

For the best effect Roses should be planted in mass and in this way they can be shown to greater advantage in a garden of formal outline. The design (Fig. 167) may vary greatly, depending on the garden location, individual taste, and the space at hand, but the beds should always be narrow with larger turf area. Gardens built on several levels should have one level reserved for Roses (Fig. 136). Gardens built all on the same level should have the Roses in the outside beds with the perennial beds toward the center.

POSITION

The Rose garden should be on high ground in an open situation that will allow an abundance of sunshine and a free circulation of air (Fig. 168). The garden should not be too close to large trees, the roots of which extend for some distance. A southeastern exposure is the best.

BEDS

Experience has taught us that Roses thrive best in narrow beds not more than twelve inches wide, (though up to three feet is practical,) with a turf path from two feet six inches to three feet wide between each bed (Fig. 167). The plants should be placed from twenty-four to thirty inches apart. It is a great mistake to plant Roses too far apart, a good average distance being twenty-four inches.

The broad turf area forms a pleasing setting for the Roses, quite in contrast with the usual broad beds, which are unsightly, impractical for the proper care of the plants, and a source of great aggravation when gathering the flowers.

PREPARATION OF BEDS

The beds should be very carefully prepared if the best results are to be obtained. This is even more important than a good selection of varieties. Roses like fertile, well drained soil, at least eighteen inches deep. If the soil is very heavy, affording poor drainage to the plants, the beds should be dug out deep and crushed stone or cinders placed in the bottom to carry off the excess. Although Roses should be in well drained soil they do not thrive vigorously

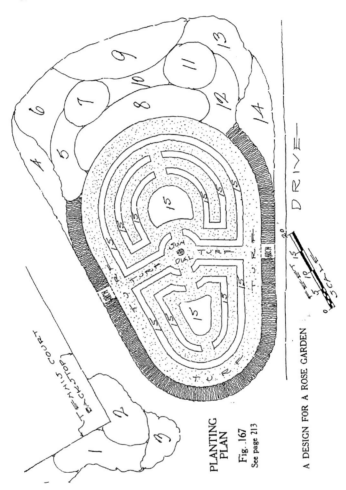

PLANTING
PLAN

Fig. 167

See page 213

A DESIGN FOR A ROSE GARDEN

KEY TO PLANTING PLAN.—Fig 167

Fig. 167.—A design for a Rose garden. Narrow beds with larger turf areas.
See pages 213, 216

Key No.	Quan.	Variety	Common Name
1	8	Spiræa Thunbergii *Escallonia or Myrta*	Snow Garland
2	8	Rosa rugosa "	Japanese Rose
3	10	Rosa Baby Rambler *Cotoneaster myers*.	Everblooming Dwarf Rose
4	8	Ligustrum lucidum *Privet. Eugenia*	Evergreen Privet
5	10	Rosa rugosa, white	White Japanese Rose
6	6	Thuya occidentalis pyramidalis	Pyramidal Arborvitæ
7	8	Rosa rugosa Ferdinand Myers *prostipuls*	Pink Japanese Rose
8	30	Rosa multiflora	White Rose
9	8	Juniperus Schottii	Pyramidal Cedar
10	12	Rosa, Harrison's Yellow	Yellow Bush Rose
11	8	Rosa rugosa Mme. Bruant	Double White Japanese Rose
12	10	Rosa rugosa, red	Red Japanese Rose
13	6	Thuya occidentalis pyramidalis	Pyramidal Arborvitæ
14	8	Ligustrum lucidum	Evergreen Privet
15	150	Hybrid tea Roses	Everblooming Roses

in very light soils. A good loam, well enriched with cow manure, will produce splendid flowers.

PLANTING AND CARE

Fall or very early Spring is the best planting season for dormant plants. If plants started in pots are secured they may be set any time after May first. The plants should receive frequent cultivation during the Summer. An abundance of water will help greatly in getting best results, so that, if possible, water should be piped to the Rose garden for convenience. Frequent spraying of the foliage with water is an aid in keeping insect pests in control. Spraying should be done in the morning, so that the foliage will be dry by night.

If the plants are robust and healthy, the result of favorable conditions, insect pests are not a serious menace.

Green fly and aphis are most prevalent. These are easily controlled by spraying with tobacco water. Leaf eating insects may be kept under control by occasional sprayings with arsenate of lead, eight ounces to five gallons of water, applied to the under side of the foliage. For mildew apply sulphate of potassium, one-half ounce to one gallon of water.

The proper pruning of the plants will depend largely on the type. The two principal types to be met in gardens are the so-called hybrid tea or everblooming Roses, and the hybrid perpetuals or June Roses.

Hybrid tea Roses should be cut back severely; the strong shoots should be cut to within twelve inches of the ground and the weak shoots removed entirely.

Hybrid perpetuals or June Roses are much stronger growing. To insure the best individual blooms the strong shoots should be cut back within a foot of the base. A less severe pruning will suffice where quantity of bloom is desired.

All pruning should be done very early in the Spring.

Roses may be successfully protected from severe Winters by a mounding of soil around the base. The entire bed should have a light mulching with coarse manure or straw. Too heavy a mulch is dangerous, as it induces growth to start too early in the Spring.

VARIETIES

As before stated, the two types of Roses most generally used in the Rose garden are the hybrid tea Roses and the hybrid perpetual Roses.

Fig. 168.—Roses well placed on a heavy soil. The drainage is excellent, and the elevation of the beds, ascending from the public road, produces a most satisfying picture when plants are in bloom. The series of unbroken lines are somewhat monotonous and could be improved by setting posts at intervals to support climbing Roses.—See page 213

Fig. 169.—Rose arches clothed with hardy climbing Roses may often be successfully
introduced into the Rose garden.—See page 219

The hybrid tea Roses are popularly known as monthly or ever-blooming sorts. They are most satisfying for garden purposes, as they are usually of neat habit with pleasing foliage and fragrant flowers, in many delicate and beautiful colors. There are so many varieties to choose from now, that a selection must depend largely on the taste of the individual. For the guidance of those unfamiliar with such plants I will name this brief selection of dependable varieties: General MacArthur, crimson red; Laurent Carle, carmine; Farben Konigin, pink; Killarney, pink; Harry Kirk, a yellow tea Rose; Lady Hillingdon, a yellow tea Rose; Kaiserin Augusta Victoria, white.

The hybrid perpetuals or June Roses make a splendid showing in June when the plants are in full bloom. After that they have but a scattering bloom during August and September. A few of the best varieties are Frau Karl Druschki, white; General Jacqueminot, crimson; Ulrich Brunner, cherry red; Mrs. R. Sharman-Crawford, deep pink; Magna Charta, bright pink.

There are numerous reliable Rose specialists throughout the country from whom catalogues should be obtained and varieties studied out in order that a satisfactory selection be made.

CLIMBING ROSES

Rose arches (Fig. 169) and Rose chains may often be very successfully introduced into the Rose garden. These should be clothed with the hardy climbing Roses, of which there is a large selection to choose from. Climbing Roses should be given plenty of space so that they may freely develop. To get the best results with climbers the question of pruning is very important. The plants should be cut back just as soon as the flowering season has passed, cutting out the old flowering shoots and leaving the young growth to develop. June and July are the months when climbing Roses are at their best, and the floral treatment of the garden should be so designed that this wealth of bloom and color may be taken advantage of to the fullest extent. These varieties are recommended: Carmine Pillar, single carmine with white center, early; Hiawatha, ruby carmine with white center; Crimson Rambler, crimson double; Dorothy Perkins, double pink; Christine Wright, double pink; Dr. Van Fleet, flesh pink; Alberic Barbier, a double pure white; Gloire de Dijon, white shaded with salmon, rather tender; Tausendschön, semi-double pink.

Fig. 170.—The wild garden will appear best in a depression where it is practicable to plant the side slopes with evergreens and flowering shrubs in a naturalistic way.—See page 221

CHAPTER X

WILD GARDENS

The wild garden, as the name suggests, is a garden of informal outline, but it is not, as many think, a wilderness, requiring little or no attention. The primary purpose of the garden is flowers, and if success is to be looked for there must be a degree of care and regard bestowed upon it, although when the garden is once established this care may be reduced to a minimum.

A wild garden consists of a collection of plants, perennials and shrubs, placed so nearly in their original environment that they become established and in great measure take care of themselves.

Very often an entire property is developed along naturalistic lines, aiming toward the picturesque in landscape design. Such a development may not be classed as a wild garden, as very often the effects secured are the result of almost constant care.

THE WILD GARDEN AS AN ISOLATED FEATURE

The true wild garden should be treated as an isolated feature and will appear best in a depression (Fig. 170) where it is practicable to plant the side slopes with evergreens and flowering shrubs in a naturalistic way. When boulders are at hand it may be made even more picturesque by placing them on the slopes and extending the plantations of wild flowers around them to tie the entire scene together.

Where space admits the plot given over to the wild garden should be large enough to allow the greatest freedom in the modification of the ground; walks should lead through depressions, the slopes of which may be built up with the earth excavated from them.

Very often a favorably located spring will supply running water and add a feature of inestimable worth to the wild garden. Many and varied are the native plants that can then be introduced and charming indeed the effects procurable.

The wild garden should be so designed that the scenes are ever changing; the paths should follow the running water, through dense, cool, shaded places, where ferns and mosses thrive, and again through open, sunny, meadow-like spaces where Buttercups and Daisies abound.

WALKS

In the wild garden the paths should be of turf (Fig. 171) or stepping stones, and very broad, allowing the flowers to sprawl over the path in places without interfering entirely with the purpose of the walk. Stepping stones should be placed twenty inches apart, center to center.

BEDS

Beds for the establishing of flowers should not be more than six feet wide. Where it is necessary to have them of greater width, it is preferable to place shrubbery in the center of the bed and to allow about three feet between the shrubbery and the turf edge of the path.

PLANTING IN THE WILD GARDEN

The proper planting of the wild garden will require an intimate knowledge of plants and a fine sense of fitness. The proper planting relates not only to the colonies of the smaller flowers that border the walks and the edges of streams, but also to the trees, shrubs and evergreens needed to make up the scene. Trees and shrubs should be selected which will supply the overhanging branches desired in places without encroaching on the open meadow-like sunny spots.

Many plants, such as the Foxgloves and Cardinal Flowers that are given places in the regular flower garden, are equally at home in the wild garden, but plants such as Geraniums and Scarlet Sage, which are peculiarly garden plants, have no place in it.

FLOWERS IN THE WILD GARDEN

As in the flower garden, the aim should be toward continuity of bloom. There should be no lack of flowers at any time, although the Spring and Fall seasons will be greatly to the fore. In this respect great aid may be looked for from the free use of hardy bulbs. Nothing is quite so pretty as colonies of Snowdrops, Jonquils, Daffodils, and similar bulbs, thoroughly naturalized.

Splendid color effects may be secured by very simple combinations of plants in the wild garden. These may be copied closely from

Fig. 171.—In the wild garden the paths should be of turf and very broad.—See page 222

nature, or be the result of individual taste in colors and color combinations.

ROCK GARDENS

GARDEN LOCATIONS

The Alpine or rock garden is closely akin to the wild garden, as here, too, we endeavor to establish plants as nearly as possible in their native environment. The Rock Garden should be apart and secluded from the Flower Garden. If it is possible to select a place where there is running water it will greatly enlarge the variety of plants that may be grown and increase the possibilities.

PLACING OF ROCKS

The rocks should be placed on a gentle slope and the surface so varied that the contour will be undulating. A few large rocks are better than many small ones. When placing the rocks adopt a plan of stratification so that the strata all run in the same direction. Secure the largest boulders possible and arrange them so that the

Fig. 172.—A dry retaining wall with pockets for plants, where the water feature adds greatly to the scene.—See page 226

most formidable stones come at the base. In some places the arrangement should be almost perpendicular and in others flattened out to a more gentle slope. In this class of work we are imitating Nature just as closely as possible and the boulders must be so arranged as to appear inherent in the soil.

SOIL

An abundance of good porous soil must be used and well mixed with leaf mold and well rotted manure to a depth of two or three feet. It is almost impossible to establish and grow a good assortment of rock plants on many of the so-called rockeries for the reason that the pockets for soil are far too small and devoid of moisture, so that only the very hardiest of drought resisting Alpines can exist.

ARRANGEMENT OF PLANTS

The arrangement of the plants should be in clumps or colonies of one variety, and not of a mixed planting where the strongest grow-

DRY WALL GARDENING

Fig. 173.—In dry wall construction the large stones should be placed at the base, and the face of the wall battered back two or three inches to the foot. Pockets of generous dimensions should be provided for the plants, and all the stones should have an inclination toward the bank. In the illustration the plants consist of Armeria, Phlox, Dianthus, Aquilegia and Epimedium.—See page 226

ing kinds can overrun the weaker, many of which would soon perish under these conditions.

MOISTURE IMPORTANT

When a rock garden is constructed on a dry hill it should be provided with a sub-irrigation system, as many Alpine plants require a deep, moist soil. This is very much more important than the shade or partial shade so often thought necessary to their well doing. Such a system of irrigation may be economically installed by running a two-inch agricultural tile along the top of the slope, twelve inches below the surface. The bottom of the trench should be inclined toward the rockery and filled with crushed stone or clean cinders, placed around the tile. The tile should be connected with a rubber hose at the faucet. The use of valves is thus done away with, such

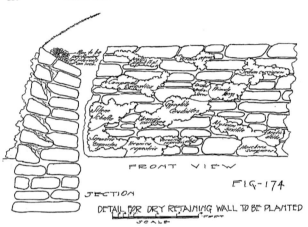

Fig. 174.—Dry stone wall with pockets for planting. Note system for watering.

as would be necessary if the line was directly connected with the water supply system. Where the rock garden is close enough to the house, water may be applied directly by hose, but the irrigation method is to be preferred.

An interesting use of rock and Alpine plants is in the planting of dry walls (Figs. 172 and 173) and particularly when such walls are built as retaining walls in the flower garden. A great variety of plants may be had for such a purpose and the list greatly enlarged if a water supply is near by to help out in very dry periods.

When it is purposed to plant the interstices in dry walls, the walls should have a batter (Fig. 174) of three inches to the foot, or one foot in a wall four feet high. The stones should be set at a right angle to the inclined line. The pockets left for plants should continue directly or indirectly through the wall so that the soil will be in direct contact with that at the back of the wall. These soil pockets should be filled as the wall progresses and the soil held in place by tough pieces of sod until ready for planting.

For wall gardens it is advisable to install a sub-irrigation system (Fig. 174) to supply abundant moisture to the wall

ANOTHER FORM OF ALPINE GARDENING

Fig. 175.—Rustic garden steps such as these should have six-inch risers and treads of not less than fourteen inches. The larger stones should be used for the base, and the soil well rammed to prevent settling. The treads should be tied into the cheek walls. In rustic work the cheek walls may be left without coping.

plants; this may be done by installing a perforated wrought iron pipe along the top at the rear of the wall; the perforation should be a thirty-second of an inch in diameter, spaced at intervals of one inch. The pipe should be placed with the holes at the bottom, on a bed of crushed stone, seven inches below the surface, and covered with three inches of cinders, allowing four inches of top soil above. The water supply should be controlled by a valve set flush with the grade, in a neat box, and located at a convenient point.

GARDEN STEPS WITH POCKETS FOR PLANTS

Garden steps of field stone (Fig. 175) in fashion with the retaining walls may be so constructed as to leave pockets for the planting of Alpines. Following a first principle of wall construction, such steps should be as regular as possible, not in absolutely straight lines, but the structure in general should be regular and uniform. This regularity should not be followed in the planting;

Fig. 176.—Stone steps making an interesting approach to the rock garden. Large field stones form the treads with earth risers. Sedum acre (Wall Pepper) is planted between the stones.—See page 229

Fig. 177.—Small, compact growing shrubs are introduced into a rock garden not only for their floral beauty, but to add stability.—See page 230

on the contrary, it may be very much varied. An important consideration in the building of such steps is stability. Large, heavy stones should be selected for the base and placed on a firm foundation. As the other stones are placed they should all lie firmly and the soil between be well rammed to prevent too much settling. The planting may usually be done as the work is in progress; the plants will then be better placed, the roots spread more easily. The pockets for plants should be so made as to prevent the crushing of the roots as the work progresses. Plants that show to best advantage on a flat surface should be given the preference, but in not too great a variety. Plants suitable are Rock Cress (*Arabis albida*), Wall Pepper (*Sedum acre.*—Fig. 176), Bugle (*Ajuga repens*), Harebell (*Campanula rotundifolia*), Soapwort (*Saponaria ocymoides*) and Speedwell (*Veronica rupestris*).

TIME OF PLANTING

Great care should be taken in planting Alpines or many failures will result. Late Spring is the very best season for planting and if it is possible to secure small potted plants they are more easily handled. Planting and building may often be done at the same time and this is advisable where possible.

SHRUBS IN ROCK GARDENS

The introduction of small, compact growing shrubs will give an appearance of stability to the rockery and deter the eye from taking in too much at a time. Many of the hardy heaths are suitable for this purpose, as are also the Andromedas, Azaleas (Fig. 177), Daphnes, Dwarf Rhododendrons and Cotoneasters.

EVERGREENS IN THE ROCK GARDEN

Coniferous evergreens should be used sparingly in the rock garden. The tall, upright types are not in keeping, and all those with golden or silvery foliage should be omitted. Some of the dwarf Junipers, such as J. tamariscifolia and J. sabina prostrata, are useful, as are the dwarf Spruces such as Picea Remonti, and the dwarf Retinisporas as Retinispora obtusa nana.

THE HEATHERS

The hardy heaths bloom from April until July. The first to bloom is Erica mediterranea. This variety makes its flower buds in the Summer and blooms the following April and May. Other hardy kinds are E. Tetralix, E. cinerea, E. vagans, E. ciliaris and Calluna vulgaris.

Used in the rock garden the heaths should be planted in clumps rather than as individual plants. A rather peaty soil should be provided and the plants placed close together, protecting the roots from wind and undue exposure.

CHAPTER XI

PLANTING PLANS AND KEYS THERETO

The plans illustrated on the following pages are mostly of properties which have been developed as planned and, though they will not apply to other plots in every detail, they may be readily adjusted to conform to grounds of a similar size.

The garden plans may be easily adopted where the area is at hand to accommodate them and the enclosing plantations; the latter is essential, for the garden setting has much to do with its success from a pictorial point of view as well as from the privacy it affords.

When modifying the plans and making substitutions to suit one's fancy or local conditions, it will save much time and annoyance to first make a list of the plants to be used, noting their ultimate height and spread, season of blooming, and the color of the flower; such a list saves much confusion in looking up each variety in the nursery catalogues when making the plan.

In border plantations it should be borne in mind that a grouping of shrubs on level ground should never exceed more than three plants in depth (placed irregularly and not in straight rows); in a limited space two plants deep will be sufficient. More than this quantity will give a monotonous, flat appearance. On slopes, the dimensions of the individual groupings are only limited by the space or the fancy of the designer.

Most of the shrubs bloom early in the Spring or late Summer, so it is suggested that a generous quantity of perennials be included in the plantations; these latter will give a charming sequence of bloom and brighten the scene throughout the season.

For the best results in plant arrangement it is essential that we have some preconceived idea as to the placing of the material of which the scene is to be made; after the conception the next step is to develop the scheme on paper, in a comprehensive manner, drawn to an accurate scale, so that it may readily be reproduced on the ground. The eraser should be used unsparingly, for it is only by the process of elimination that we finally realize the best

KEY TO PLAN "A" OPPOSITE

Key No.	Quan.	Variety	Common Name
1	3	Syringa Charles X	Lilac
2	1	Kerria japonica (single)	Corchorus
3	4	Hydrangea arborescens grandiflora	
4	5		Hills of Snow
5	3	Buddleia Veitchiana	Butterfly Shrub
6	2	Spiraea Van Houttei	Van Houttes' Spirea
7	5	Hibiscus Lady Stanley	Rose of Sharon
8	4	Spiraea Anthony Waterer	Waterer's Spirea
9	4	Weigela rosea	Pink Weigela
10	3	Syringa Marie Legraye	White Lilac
11	3	Viburnum tomentosum	Single Japanese Snowball
12	3	Philadelphus, Avalanche	Mock Orange
13	5	Berberis purpurea	Purple Barberry
14	2	Kerria japonica fl. pl.	Corchorus
15	4	Berberis Thunbergii	Japanese Barberry
16	3	Spiraea Van Houttei	Van Houtte's Spirea
17	1	Salisburia adiantifolia	Maidenhair Tree
18	7	Hypericum Moserianum	St. John's Wort
19	7	Berberis Thunbergii	Japanese Barberry
20	1	Laburnum vulgare	Golden Chain
21	6	Deutzia gracilis	Dwarf Deutzia
22	7	Abelia grandiflora	Hybrid Abelia
23	4	Cercis japonica	Japanese Red Bud
24	5	Stephanandra flexuosa	
25	1	Hibiscus coelestis	Rose of Sharon
26	3	Caragana arborescens	Siberian Pea
27	1	Hibiscus Carnation stripe	Rose of Sharon
27½	50	Berberis Thunbergii (Hedge 18 in. apart)	Japanese Barberry
28	38	Cotoneaster Simonsii	Shining leaved Cotoneaster
29	1	Deutzia Lemoinei	Lemoine's Deutzia
30	1	Hibiscus coelestis	Rose of Sharon
31	9	Abelia grandiflora	Hybrid Abelia
32	8	Hydrangea arborescens grandiflora	Hills of Snow
33	8	Berberis Thunbergii	Japanese Barberry
34	1	Quercus rubra	Red Oak
35	7	Ligustrum Regelianum	Regel's Privet
36	1	Laburnum vulgare	Golden Chain
37	6	Symphoricarpos racemosus	Snowberry
38	4	Deutzia gracilis	Dwarf Deutzia
39	1	Viburnum tomentosum	Single Japanese Snowball
40	3	Forsythia viridissima	Golden Bell
41	5	Hydrangea paniculata grandiflora	Large flowered Hydrangea
42	1	Magnolia Soulangeana	Pink Magnolia
43	4	Weigela rosea	Pink Weigela
44	1	Cornus florida rubra	Pink Dogwood
44½	3	Deutzia Pride of Rochester	Pink Deutzia
45	1	Deutzia crenata	White Deutzia
46	5	Kerria japonica (single)	Corchorus
47	3	Syringa Mme. Lemoine	White Lilac
48	3	Buddleia Veitchiana	Butterfly Shrub
49	1	Exochorda grandiflora	Pearl Bush
49½	2	Caryopteris Mastacanthus	Verbena Shrub
50	2	Viburnum oxycoccos	High Bush Cranberry
51	3	Syringa Ludwig Spaeth	Lilac
52	5	Berberis purpurea	Purple Barberry
53	3	Symphoricarpos vulgaris	Indian Currant
54	4	Berberis Thunbergii	Japanese Barberry
55	5	Kerria japonica, single	Corchorus
56	3	Hollyhocks, pink.	
57	5	Peonia Festiva Maxima	White Peony
58	3	Caragana arborescens	Siberian Pea
59	1	Rhus Cotinus	Smoke Tree
60	3	Tamarix hispida estivalis	Tamarisk
61	2	Hypericum prolificum	Aaron's Beard
62	5	Philadelphus, Avalanche	Mock Orange
63	3	Spiraea, Van Houttei	Van Houtte's Spirea
64	6	Berberis Thunbergii	Japanese Barberry
65	3	Azalea amoena	Evergreen Azalea
66	5	Philadelphus coronarius	Mock Orange
67	5	Daphne Genkwa	Japanese Daphne
68	3	Rosa rubiginosa	Sweet Briar
69	10	Chrysanthemum (pink, white and yellow varieties)	
70	7	Digitalis purpurea	Foxglove
71	10	Iris Kaempferi	Japanese Flag
72	6	Delphinium elatum	Larkspur
73	2	Rosa rubiginosa	Pink Rose
74	5	Rosa Ferdinand Meyer	Sweet Briar
74½	12	Delphinium hybridum	Larkspur
75	10	Iris pallida dalmatica	Flag
76	1	Chrysanthemum Boston	Yellow Chrysanthemum
77	2	Baptisia australis	False Indigo
78	12	Chrysanthemum Soleil d'Or	Yellow Chrysanthemum
79	10	Phlox Elizabeth Campbell	Pink Phlox
80	10	Iris Kaempferi	Japanese Flag
81	5	Azalea Hino-de-giri	Evergreen Japanese Azalea
82	15	Iris Louis Van Houttei	Flag
83	7	Berberis Thunbergii	Japanese Barberry
84	5	Philadelphus, Avalanche	Mock Orange
85	5	Spiraea Thunbergii	Thunberg's Spirea
86	1	Viburnum plicatum	Japanese Snowball
87	1	Spiraea prunifolia fl. pl.	Bridal Wreath
88	5	Viburnum Carlesii	Pink Viburnum
89	1	Magnolia purpurea	Purple Viburnum
90	3	Forsythia viridissima	Golden Bell
91	1	Berberis purpurea	Purple Barberry
92	3	Viburnum Opulus sterilis	Snowberry
93	3	Liquidambar styraciflua	Sweet Gum

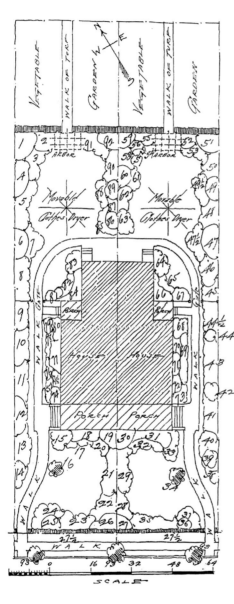

PLANTING PLAN
"A"

On this plan, representing a width of 80 ft. by a depth of 200 ft. stand two semi-detached houses.

The entire boundary is arranged in plantations of shrubbery and are of such varieties as will give a sequence of bloom from early Spring until late Fall, followed by a little interest of color in the berry bearing plants, such as the Barberry, Coral Berry, Snowberry and Cotoneaster.

The perennials are placed along the base of the house, and the varieties suggested, while limited, will provide a goodly quantity of cut flowers for table decoration.

The front lawns may be treated as one lawn to advantage by omitting numbers 21 and 29, while the rear, for reasons of privacy, is better enclosed by the shrub borders.

A small vegetable garden is placed at the rear, separated by a hedge, which will also form a background to the plantations in front of it.

Between the rear lawn and the vegetable garden a small arbor is suggested in which seats may be placed at the sides.

Either climbing Roses, Clematis or annual vines should be planted as the decoration for the arbor.

For laundry purposes a movable drier is indicated in the center of the grass plot. This is easily put up and taken down as occasion may require, and is infinitely better than the unsightly posts.

On the scale given below the plan 16 equals 8 ft.; 32 equals 16 ft.; 64 equals 32 ft.

KEY TO PLAN "B"

Key No.	Quan.	Variety	Common Name
1	3	Pyracantha coccinea Leland	Evergreen Thorn
2	5	Abelia grandiflora	Hybrid Abelia
3	3	Cornus florida rubra	Pink Dogwood
4	3	Cotoneaster Simonsii	Shiny leaved Cotoneaster
5	3	Enkianthus japonica	
6	3	Azalea ledifolium var. leucanthemum	Evergreen White Azalea
7	6	Mahonia aquifolia	Oregon Grape
8	1	Cedrus Deodora	Himalayan Cedar
9	3	Laurustinus Tinus	
10	3	Cotoneaster Augustifolia	
11	3	Nandina japonica	Heavenly Bamboo
12	7	Iris Kæmpferi	Japanese Flag
13	1	Camellia japonica	Camellia
14	5	Pæonia Festiva Maxima	White Peony
15	1	Spiræa Van Houtei	Van Houtte's Spiræa
16	8	Phlox G. A. Strohlein	Orange Red Phlox
17	1	Viburnum tomentosum	Single Japanese Snowball
18	8	Delphinium hybridum	Larkspur
19	1	Amygdalus nana	Flowering Almond
20	8	Phlox Elizabeth Campbell	Pink Phlox
21	1	Deutzia Lemoinei	Lemoine's Deutzia
22	3	Hydrangea Hortensis (blue)	
23	10	Chrysanthemum Jardin des Plantes	White Chrysanthemum
24	6	Thalictrum Dipterocarpum	Meadow Rue
25	6	Eupatorium coelestinum	Hardy Ageratum
26	9	Chrysanthemum maximum	Shasta Daisy
27	1	Robinia hispida	Moss Locust
28	3	Abelia grandiflora	Hybrid abelia
29	3	Mahonia japonica	Japanese Evergreen Barberry
30	3	Ilex crenata – acrepholia.	Japanese Holly
31	3	Ilex crenata	Japanese Holly
32	3	Mahonia aquifolia	Oregon grape
33	3	Jasminum nudiflorum	Jasmine
34	8	Bocconia cordata	Plume Poppy
35	4	Ilex aquifolia	English Holly
36	20	Abelia grandiflora	Hybrid Abelia
37	2	Taxus hibernica	Irish Yew
38	1	Camellia japonica	Camellia
39	1	Ceanothus Gloire de Versailles	
40	6	Pæonia rubro-plena	Red Peony
41	10	Phlox Wm. Robinson	Pink Phlox
42	10	Delphinium hybridum	Larkspur
43	1	Spiræa arguta	
44	10	Iris Kæmpferi	Japanese Flag
45	1	Berberis purpurea	Purple Barberry
46	10	Chrysanthemum Henry Sesquier	Violet Rose Chrysanthemum
47	1	Forsythia viridissima	Golden Bell
47½	10	Phlox Elizabeth Campbell	Pink Phlox
48	1	Syringa Mme. Lemoine	White Lilac
49	18	Hypericum calcynum	Aaron's Beard
50	4	Nandina japonica	Heavenly Bamboo
51	5	Rhododendron Parsons Gloriosa	Rose Bay
52	7	Aucuba japonica green	Japanese Laurel
53	4	Genista juncea	Spanish Broom
54	8	Hydrangea arborescens grandiflora	Hills of Snow
55	1	Cedrus Deodara	Himalayan Cedar
56		Quercus coccinea	Scarlet Oak
57		Cornus florida rubra	Pink Dogwood
58		Ulmus americana	American Elm
59		Cedrela sinensis	

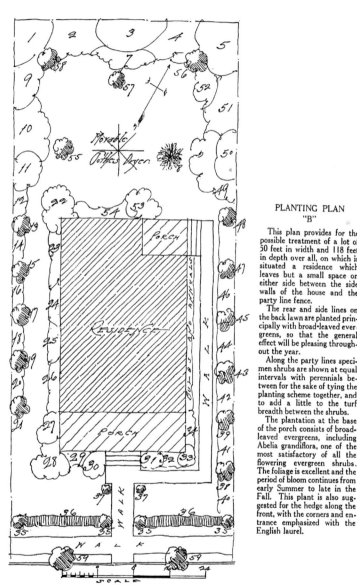

PLANTING PLAN "B"

This plan provides for the possible treatment of a lot of 50 feet in width and 118 feet in depth over all, on which is situated a residence which leaves but a small space on either side between the side walls of the house and the party line fence.

The rear and side lines on the back lawn are planted principally with broad-leaved evergreens, so that the general effect will be pleasing throughout the year.

Along the party lines specimen shrubs are shown at equal intervals with perennials between for the sake of tying the planting scheme together, and to add a little to the turf breadth between the shrubs.

The plantation at the base of the porch consists of broad-leaved evergreens, including Abelia grandiflora, one of the most satisfactory of all the flowering evergreen shrubs. The foliage is excellent and the period of bloom continues from early Summer to late in the Fall. This plant is also suggested for the hedge along the front, with the corners and entrance emphasized with the English laurel.

KEY TO PLAN "C"

Key No.	Quan.	Variety	Common Name
1	47	Hybrid Tea Roses	
2	4	{ Cratægus, Double white Cratægus, alba } plena Double red, Paul's Scarlet }	Hawthorn
3	4	Salisburia adiantifolia	Maidenhair Tree
4	3	Abelia grandiflora	Hybrid Abelia
5	1	Buddleia Veitchiana	Butterfly shrub
6	7	Bocconia cordata	Plume Poppy
7	10	Delphinium hybridum	Larkspur
8	10	Phlox Mrs. Jenkins	White Phlox
9	10	Phlox Elizabeth Campbell	Pink Phlox
10	7	Pæonia Festiva Maxima	White Peony
11	1	Spiræa Van Houttei	Van Houtte's Spiræa
12	1	Abelia grandiflora	Hybrid Abelia
13	1	Mahonia aquifolia	Oregon Grape
14	1	Aucuba japonica	Japanese Laurel
15	1	Cotoneaster Simonsii	Shiny-leaved Cotoneaster
16	1	Mahonia japonica	Japanese Evergreen Barberry
17	2	Juniperus hibernica	Irish Juniper
18	5	Retinispora obtusa	Japanese Cypress
19	1	Thuyopsis dolobrata	
20	16	Retinispora squarrosa Veitchii	Japanese Blue Cypress
21	2	Acer saccharum	Sugar Maple
22	1	Cotoneaster Simonsii	Shiny-leaved Cotoneaster
23	1	Mahonia japonica	Japanese Evergreen Barberry
24	1	Aucuba japonica	Japanese Laurel
25	1	Abelia grandiflora	Hybrid Abelia
26	1	Mahonia aquifolia	Oregon Grape
27	1	Berberis Thunbergii	Japanese Barberry
28	1	Deutzia gracilis	Dwarf Duetzia
29	1	Spiræa Anthony Waterer	Pink Spiræa
30	1	Spiræa callosa alba	Dwarf white Spiræa
31	1	Amygdalus fl. pl. rubra	Flowering Almond
32	1	Coryopteris Mastacanthus	Verbena Shrub
33	6	Buddleia magnifica	Butterfly shrub
34	5	Hydrangea arborescens grandiflora	Large-flowered Hydrangea
35	3	Thalictrum dipterocarpum	Meadow Rue
36	4	Aconitum Park's hybrids	Monkshood
37	5	Anemone Queen Charlotte	Windflower
38	15	Iris Kaempferi	Japanese Flag
39	8	Stokesia cyanea	Stokes' Aster
40	15	Iris Queen of May	Flag
41	6	Pæonia Jeanne d'Arc	Rose Colored Peony
42	11	Platycodon Mariesii	Chinese Bell Flower
43	5	Phlox Struthers	Cherry Red Phlox
44	6	Pentstemon barbatus	Beard Tongue
45	6	Iris King of Iris	Yellow Flag
46	15	Phlox Mrs. Jenkins	White Phlox
47	8	Funkia lancifolia	Plantain Lily
48	10	Chrysanthemum Henry Sesquier	Violet Rose Shades
49	6	Pæonia Charlemagne's	White Peony
50	10	Campanula calycanthema	Bell Flower
51	10	Chrysanthemum Jardin des Plantes	White Chrysanthemum
52	6	Pæonia lutea variegata	Pink Peony
53	15	Iris Kaempferi	Japanese Flag
54	12	Platycodon Mariesii	Chinese Bellflower
55	8	Stokesia cyanea	Stokes' Aster
56	5	Aquilegia cærulea	Columbine
56½	4	Aconitum, Park's variety	Monkshood
57	5	Anemone Queen Charlotte	Windflower
58	6	Pæonia Festiva Maxima	White Peony
59	10	Chrysanthemum Jardin des Plantes	White Chrysanthemum
60	15	Phlox Elizabeth Campbell	Pink Phlox
61	10	Campanula latifolia macrantha	Bellflower
62	7	Pæonia Cytharee	Flesh White Peony
63	6	Iris pallida dalmatica	Blue Flag
64	6	Pentstemon barbatus	Beard Tongue
95	5	Phlox Miss Lingard	White Phlox

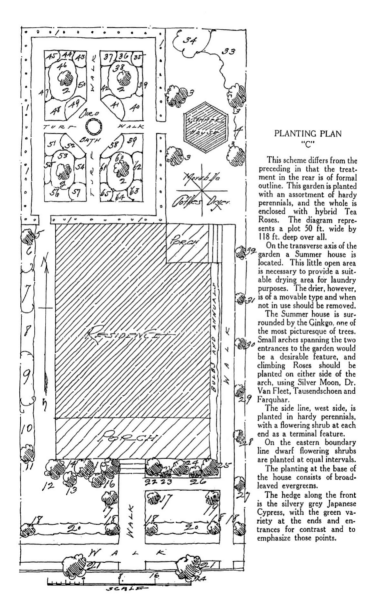

PLANTING PLAN "C"

This scheme differs from the preceding in that the treatment in the rear is of formal outline. This garden is planted with an assortment of hardy perennials, and the whole is enclosed with hybrid Tea Roses. The diagram represents a plot 50 ft. wide by 118 ft. deep over all.

On the transverse axis of the garden a Summer house is located. This little open area is necessary to provide a suitable drying area for laundry purposes. The drier, however, is of a movable type and when not in use should be removed.

The Summer house is surrounded by the Ginkgo, one of the most picturesque of trees. Small arches spanning the two entrances to the garden would be a desirable feature, and climbing Roses should be planted on either side of the arch, using Silver Moon, Dr. Van Fleet, Tausendschoen and Farquhar.

The side line, west side, is planted in hardy perennials, with a flowering shrub at each end as a terminal feature.

On the eastern boundary line dwarf flowering shrubs are planted at equal intervals.

The planting at the base of the house consists of broad-leaved evergreens.

The hedge along the front is the silvery grey Japanese Cypress, with the green variety at the ends and entrances for contrast and to emphasize those points.

KEY TO PLAN "D"

Key No.	Quan.	Variety	Common Name
1	1	Syringa Charles X	Lilac
2	15	Iris Kaempferi	Japanese Flag
3	10	Paeonia Festiva Maxima	White Peony
4	16	Helianthus Miss Willmott	Sunflower
5	14	Phlox Athis	Pink Phlox
6	1	Ligustrum lucidum	Evergreen Privet
7	7	Physostegia virginica	False Dragon's Head
8	12	Chrysanthemum Jardin des Plantes	Yellow Flowered
9	15	Fuchsia elegans	Pink Phlox
10	20	Phlox Mrs. Campbell	Larkspur
11	15	Delphinium Mrs. Thompson	White Lilac
12	12	Syringa Frau Bertha Dammon	Giant Diasy
13	12	Pyrethrum uliginosum	Pyramidal Box
14	2	Buxus pyramidalis	False Chamomile
15	10	Boltonia asteroides	Japanese Flag
16	15	Iris Kaempferi	Lilac
17	1	Syringa Michael Bushner	Pink Peony
18	10	Paeonia Jeanne d'Arc	Snapdragon
19	10	Antirrhinum, pink	Red Phlox
20	14	Phlox R. P. Struthers	Yellow and Blue Flag
21	10	Iris Niebelungen	Stoke's Aster
22	15	Stokesia cyanea	Hybrid Abelia
23	1	Abelia grandiflora	Bellflower
24	1	Campanula persicifolia	Hybrid Abelia
25	16	Abelia grandiflora	Pink Phlox
26	1	Phlox Wm. Robinson	Gold and Pearl Flag
27	8	Iris Gypsy Queen	Chinese Bellflower
28	10	Platycodon Mariesii	Larkspur
29	15	Delphinium hybridum	Lilac
30	1	Syringa Pres. Grevy	Shasta Daisy Alaska
31	12	Chrysanthemum maximum	Blue Aster
32	12	Aster novæ-angliæ pulchella	Pyramidal Box
33	2	Buxus pyramidalis	Flesh colored Climbing Rose
34	1	Rosa Dr. Van Fleet	Pink Rose
35	1	Rosa Tausendschoen	Pink Rose
36	1	Rosa Gloire de Dijon	Yellow Rose
37	1	Rosa Alberic Barbier	Mock Orange
38	1	Philadelphus, Avalanche	
39		Bulbs and Annuals	
40	1	Spiræa Aitchisoni	
41	4	Stephanandra Tanakee	Corchorus
42	8	Kerria japonica	Lemoine's Deutzia
43	5	Deutzia Lemoinei	
44	5	Hydrangea arborescens grandiflora	Hills of Snow
45	4	Viburnum Carlesii	Pink Viburnum
46	3	Thuya pyramidalis	Pyramidal Arborvite
47	20	Berberis Thunbergii	Japanese Barberry
48	2	Thuya pyramidalis	Pyramidal Arborvite
49	1	Osmanthus aquifolium	Holly-leaved Tea Olive
50	1	Abelia grandiflora	Hybrid Abelia
51	1	Genista juncea	Spanish Broom
52	1	Jasminum nudiflorum	Jasmine
53	1	Abelia grandiflora	Hybrid Abelia
54	1	Lycium barbarum	Washington's Bower
55	1	Jasminum nudiflorum	Jasmine
56	1	Lycium barbarum	Washington's Bower
57	1	Jasminum nudiflorum	Jasmine
58	1	Abelia grandiflora	Hybrid Abelia
59	1	Genista juncea	Spanish Broom
60	5	Paeonia chrysanthemiflora	White Peony
61	1	Forsythia intermedia	Golden Bell
62	1	Abelia grandiflora	Hybrid Abelia
63	1	Ilex aquifolium	English Holly
64	1	Abelia grandiflora	Hybrid Abelia
65	1	Ilex aquifolium	English Holly
66	1	Abelia grandiflora	Hybrid Abelia
67	1	Photinia serrulata	Evergreen Photinia
68	1	Abelia grandiflora	Hybrid Abelia
69	8	Hollyhocks	Pink and Yellow
70	1	Ilex aquifolium	English Holly
71	1	Digitalis purpurea	Foxglove
72	1	Abelia grandiflora	Hybrid Abelia
73	7	Delphinium Kelway's hybrids	Larkspur
74	7	Ilex aquifolium	English Holly
75	10	Phlox R. P. Struthers	Red Phlox
76	2	Platanus orientalis	Oriental Plane

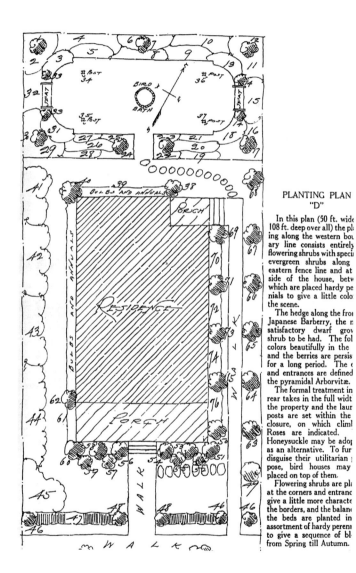

PLANTING PLAN
"D"

In this plan (50 ft. wide
108 ft. deep over all) the pl
ing along the western bou
ary line consists entirely
flowering shrubs with speci
evergreen shrubs along
eastern fence line and at
side of the house, betw
which are placed hardy pe
nials to give a little colo
the scene.

The hedge along the fro
Japanese Barberry, the n
satisfactory dwarf grov
shrub to be had. The fol
colors beautifully in the
and the berries are persis
for a long period. The
and entrances are defined
the pyramidal Arborvitæ.

The formal treatment in
rear takes in the full widt
the property and the laur
posts are set within the
closure, on which climl
Roses are indicated.
Honeysuckle may be ado;
as an alternative. To fur
disguise their utilitarian ;
pose, bird houses may
placed on top of them.

Flowering shrubs are pl;
at the corners and entranc
give a little more characte
the borders, and the balan
the beds are planted in
assortment of hardy peren:
to give a sequence of bl
from Spring till Autumn.

KEY TO PLAN "E"

Key No.	Quan.	Variety	Common Name
1	1	Retinispora obtusa, Japanese Cypress	
2	1	Jasminum officinalis, Jasmine	
3	1	Juniperus Pfitzeriana	
4	1	Juniperus tamariscifolia	
5	1	Thuya Warreana, Siberian Arborvitæ	
6	1	Clematis coccinea, Scarlet Clematis	
7	1	Juniperus Sabina compacta	
8	1	Retinispora squarrosa Veitchii, Japanese Blue Cypress	
9	1	Clematis paniculata, Japanese Clematis	
10	1	Juniperus japonica aurea, Japanese Golden Juniper	
11	1	Thuya vervaeneana, Golden Arborvitæ	
12	1	Jasminum primulinum, Yellow Jasmine	
13	1	Retinispora obtusa, Japanese Cypress	
14	1	Juniperus Pfitzeriana	
15	1	Juniperus Waukeegan	
16	1	Juniperus canadensis aurea	
17	20	Tsuga canadensis, Hemlock Spruce	
18	21	Aesculus glabra, Horse-Chestnut	
19	8	Thuya pyramidalis, Pyramidal Arborvitæ	
20	8	Hypericum Moserianum, St. John's Wort	
21	16	Viola Blue Perfection.	
22	1	Chamaecyparis erecta viridis, Pyramidal Cypress	
23	20	Iris pumila, Dwarf Flag	
24	11	Iris Gypsy Queen, Golden Flag	
25	1	Plumbago Larpentæ, Leadwort	
26	17	Iris Kaempferi, Japanese Flag	
27	2	Heuchera sanguinea, Alum Root	
28	9	Phlox Elizabeth Campbell, Pink Phlox	
29	1	Chamaecyparis erecta viridis, Pyramidal Cypress	
30	1	Retinispora obtusa aurea, Japanese Cypress	
31	9	Juniperus Cannarti	
32	12	Stokesia cyanea, Stokes' Aster	
33	10	Phlox Miss Lingard, White Phlox	
34	7	Retinispora obtusa, Japanese Cypress	
35	14	Gaillardia grandiflora, Blanket Flower	
36	5	Phlox Mrs. Jenkins, White Phlox	
37	7	Sciadopitys verticillata, Umbrella Pine	
38	8	Hemerocallis flava, Day Lily	
39	8	Delphinium hybridum, I Larkspur	
40	1	Juniperus virginiana, Red Cedar	
41	10	Tritoma Pfitzeriana, Redhot Poker Plant	
42	7	Caleriana officinalis, Garden Heliotrope	
43	3	Boltonia asteroides, False Chamomile	
44	3	Iberis sempervirens, Candytuft	
45	1	Helianthus Miss Willmott, Sunflower	
46	1	Juniperus virginiana, Red Cedar	
47	10	Physostegia virginica, False Dragon's Head	
48	12	Platycodon Mariesii (white), Chinese Bellflower	
49	1	Juniperus Schottei	
50	2	Cerasus rosea pendula, Japanese Weeping Cherry	
51	8	Delphinium Albion, White Larkspur	
52	12	Iris flavescens, Yellow Flag	
53	8	Delphinium Lize Van Veen, Larkspur	
54	12	Pentstemon barbatus, Beard's Tongue.	
55	5	Iris Kaempferi, Japanese Flag	
56	1	Juniperus Schottei	
57	8	Heliopsis Pitcheriana semi-plena	
58	15	Polymonium Richardsoni, Jacob's Ladder	
59	5	Juniperus virginiana, Red Cedar	
60	5	Aster novæ-angliæ Roycroft, Pink Aster	
61	8	Stokesia cyanea, Stokes' Aster	
62	3	Delphinium Rev. E. Lascelles, Larkspur	
63	3	Aconitum, Park's varieties, Monkshood	
64	2	Aquilegia cærulea, Columbine	
65	1	Juniperus virginiana, Red Cedar	
66	14	Phlox R. P. Struthers, Red Phlox	
67	8	Iris Queen of May, Rose Lilac Flag	
68	5	Lavendula vera, Lavender	
69	10	Rudbeckia purpurea, Cone Flower	
70	1	Juniperus Cannarti	
71	8	Iris King of Iris, Yellow Flag	
72	7	Iris Kaempferi, Japanese Flag	
73	1	Desmodium penduliflorum, Bush Clover	
74	4	Sedum spectabile, Showy Sedum	
75	14	Achillea, The Pearl	
76	1	Pentstemon barbatus, Beard's Tongue	
77	8	Eupatorium ageratoides, White Snakeroot	
78	8	Chrysanthemum, Golden Pheasant, Yellow Chrysanthemum	
79	6	Phlox Mrs. Jenkins, White Phlox	
80	6	Stokesia cyanea, Stoke's Aster	
81	5	Inula laciniata, Fleabane	
82	3	Iris florentina, White Flag	
83	7	Hemerocallis flava, Day Lily	
84	5	Anemone Queen Charlotte, Windflower	
85	7	Paeonia Festiva Maxima, White Peony	
86	3	Boltonia latisquama, False Chamomile	
87	8	Delphinium hybridum, Larkspur	
88	7	Gypsophila paniculata, Baby's breath	
89	1	Hibiscus, Marvel Mallow	
90	5	Anchusa italica (Dropmore's) Italian Alkanet	
91	8	Iberis sempervirens, Candytuft	
92	3	Hollyhocks, Yellow	
93	4	Delphinium Albion, White Larkspur	
94	8	Platycodon Mariesii, Chinese Bellflower	
95	7	Phlox Elizabeth Campbell, Pink Phlox	
96	7	Papaver orientalis, Oriental Poppy	
97	7	Asclepias tuberosa, Butterfly weed	
98	3	Hollyhocks, Pink	
99	10	Lupinus polyphyllus (blue), Lupine	
100	8	Campanula pyramidalis, Bellflower	
101	7	Paeonia chrysanthemiflora, White Peony	
102	4	Buddleia magnifica, Butterfly Shrub	
103	1	Retinispora obtusa	
104	6	Phlox Frau Anton Buchner, White Phlox	
105	3	Aconitum, Park's varieties	
106	2	Paeonia Pottsi Rosea, Pink Peony	
107	12	Delphinium persimmon	
108	7	Hollyhocks, yellow	
109	1	Thuya pyramidalis	
110	1	Thuya pyramidalis	
111	5	Funkia japonica, Plantain Lily	
112	5	Delphinium Mrs. Thompson, Larkspur	
113	10	Chrysanthemum Mrs. Henry Secquier, Pink Chrysanthemum	
114	2	Juniperus Annarti	
115	1	Lonicera Halleana, Hall's Honeysuckle	
116	1	Lonicera brachypoda aurea, Golden Honeysuckle	
117	1	Lonicera sinensis, Chinese Honeysuckle	
118	1	Lonicera belgica, Dutch Honeysuckle	

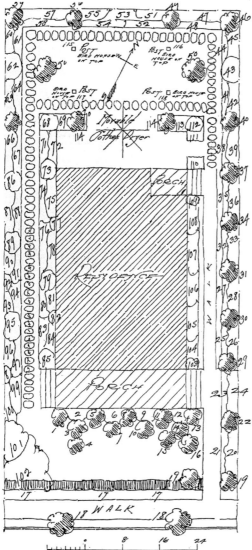

PLANTING PLAN
"E"

In this scheme the tre...
ment is of formal charact...
the only informal part bei...
in front of the porch, and t...
small plantation at the sou...
west corner. The diagram r...
resents a property 50 ft. wi...
by 108 ft. deep over all.

The stepping stone walk...
the west side is placed betw...
two borders of perennials a...
leads to the enclosure at t...
rear.

Shrubbery has been plac...
at intervals in the beds to...
them up and break the m...
notony. This feature is c...
tinued along the eastern fe...
line, while at the base of t...
house the planting is confir...
to the hardy perennials w...
the exception of two ev...
greens placed at the ends...
the beds.

The plantation in front...
the porch consists of an asso...
ment of conifers, in back...
which a variety of vines...
placed for color effect. Bu...
for Spring, followed by l...
growing annuals, would g...
an additional interest to t...
plantation.

The hedge along the fr...
is the Hemlock Spruce, anc...
should be kept at a height...
three to four feet.

KEY TO PLANTING PLAN.—Fig. 178

Key No.	Quan.	Variety	Common Name
1	7	Rhodotypos kerrioides	White Kerria
2	4	Hibiscus syriacus, single pink	Rose of Sharon
3	16	Spiræa A. Waterer	Dwarf Pink Spiræa
4	10	Lonicera fragrantissima	Early Fragrant Honeysuckle
5	12	Hydrangea paniculata (type)	Late Hydrangea
6	5	Spiræa Thunbergii	Snow Garland
7	7	Buddleia Veitchiana	Butterfly Plant
8	5	Hydrangea arborescens grandiflora alba	Hills of Snow
9	10	Lonicera Morrowi	Japanese Bush Honeysuckle
10	8	Spiræa A. Waterer	Dwarf Pink Spiræa
11	6	Yucca filamentosa	Adam's Needle
12	1	Acer saccharum	Sugar Maple
13	3	Mahonia aquifolia	Holly-leaved Barberry
14	3	Philadelphus coronarius	Mock Orange
15	6	Jasminum nudiflorum	Yellow Jasmine
16	5	Desmodium penduliflorum	Bush Clover
17	5	Rhodotypos kerrioides	White Kerria
18	5	Desmodium japonicum	White Bush Clover
19	5	Abelia grandiflora	Hybrid Abelia
20	8	Rhododendron album elegans	White Rhododendron
21	7	Azalea Hinodegiri	Japanese Evergreen Azalea
22	6	Rhododendron myrtifolium	Myrtle-leaved Rhododendron
23	5	Rhododendron John Walter	Crimson Rhododendron
23½	6	Rhododendron roseum elegans	Pink Rhododendron
24	1	Juniperus virginiana glauca	Blue Cedar
25	8	Abelia grandiflora	Hybrid Abelia
26	9	Forsythia suspensa	Weeping Golden Bell
27	5	Lonicera Morrowi	Japanese Bush Honeysuckle
28	9	Lonicera fragrantissima	Fragrant Honeysuckle
29	8	Lonicera Morrowi	Japanese Bush Honeysuckle
30	9	Forsythia suspensa	Drooping Golden Bell
31	9	Abelia grandiflora	Hybrid Abelia
32	2	Juniperus Cannarti	Cannart's Cedar
33	12	Spiræa Thunbergii	Snow Garland
34	14	Ligustrum Regelianum	Regel's Privet
35	8	Weigela Eva Rathke	Dark Red Weigela
36	9	Spiræa Van Houttei	Bridal Wreath
37	5	Caryopteris mastacanthus	Blue Spiræa
38	5	Syringa Marie Legraye	Lilac
39	8	Buddleia Veitchiana	Butterfly Plant
40	10	Hydrangea paniculata grandiflora	Large-flowered Hydrangea
41	4	Rhododendron Hybrids	
42	4	Rhododendron Hybrids	
43	5	Rhododendron Hybrids	
44	5	Rhododendron Hybrids	
45	10	Chrysanthemum Golden Mme. Martha	Yellow Chrysanthemum
46	8	Phlox Rheinlander	Pink Phlox
47	8	Hesperis matronalis	Rocket
48	8	Digitalis purpurea	Foxglove
49	10	Aster amellus, Beauty of Ronsdorf	Michaelmas Daisy
50	10	Digitalis purpurea	Foxglove
51	5	Lonicera Morrowi	Japanese Bush Honeysuckle
52	5	Lonicera Morrowi	Japanese Bush Honeysuckle
53	5	Hydrangea paniculata (type)	Panicled Hydrangea
54	5	Exochorda grandiflora	Pearl Bush
55	5	Lonicera fragrantissima	Fragrant Honeysuckle
56		Annuals and Bedding Plants	
57	15	Juniperus Schottii	Schott's Juniper
58	7	Desmodium penduliflorum	Siebold's Desmodium
59	15	Phlox Miss Lingard	Early White Phlox
60	12	Gaillardia grandiflora	Blanket Flower
61	7	Hypericum aureum	St. John's Wort
62	6	Deutzia gracilis	Slender Deutzia
63	12	Chrysanthemum St. Illoria	Pink Chrysanthemum
64	12	Phlox Elizabeth Campbell	Early Phlox
65	12	Phlox Von Lassburg	Hardy Phlox
66	4	Kerria japonica, single	Japanese Rose
67	7	Rosa rugosa	Wrinkled Japanese Rose
68	5	Spiræa Thunbergii	Snow Garland

PLANTING PLAN.—Fig. 178

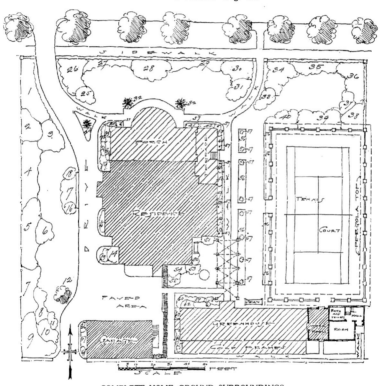

COMPLETE HOME GROUND SURROUNDINGS

Fig. 178.—Property approximately 195 feet x 165 feet. A very complete scheme including a tennis court, garage, greenhouse and coldframes. The tennis court is enclosed by a pergola and affords a space for open air theatricals, the workroom of the greenhouse providing a dressing room for the same

KEY TO PLANTING PLAN.—Fig. 179

Key No.	Quan.	Variety	Common Name
1	1	Populus fastigiata	Lombardy Poplars
2	1	Populus fastigata	Lombardy Poplars
3	1	Quercus palustris	Pin Oak
4	1	Fraxinus americana	American Ash
5	1	Acer saccharum	Sugar Maple
6	3	Salisburia adiantifolia	Maidenhair Tree
7	2	Acer polymorphum dissectum rubrum	Cut-leaved Japanese Maple
8	3	Thuya plicatum	Fern-leaved Arborvitæ
8	2	Juniperus elegantissima Leei	Golden Juniper
9	1	Liquidambar styraciflua	Sweet Gum
10	5	Viburnum tomentosum	Single Japanese Snowball
11	6	Lonicera fragrantissima	Early Bush Honeysuckle
12	5	Syringa, named varieties	Lilacs
13	5	Hydrangea paniculata	Late Hydrangea
14	6	Philadelphus coronarius	Mock Orange
15	7	Rosa rugosa	Japanese Rose
16	6	Buddleia Veitchiana	Butterfly Plant
17	5	Viburnum plicatum	Japanese Snowball
18	6	Lonicera Morrowi	Bush Honeysuckle
19	7	Abelia grandiflora	Hybrid Abelia
20	9	Rhododendron album elegans	White Rhododendron
21	8	Rhododendron roseum elegans	Pink Rhododendron
22	7	Lonicera Morrowi	Bush Honeysuckle
23	6	Rosa rugosa	Japanese Rose
24	4	Spiræa Van Houttei	Drooping Spiræa
25	5	Spiræa Thunbergii	Snow Garland
26	3	Weigela Eva Rathke	Red Weigela
27	5	Philadelphus Lemoinei	Mock Orange
28	6	Spiræa Van Houttei	Drooping Spiræa
29	6	Hydrangea paniculata grandiflora	Large flowering Hydrangea
30	8	Spiræa Thunbergii	Snow Garland
31	9	Abelia grandiflora	Hybrid Abelia
32	7	Azalea Hinodegiri	Japanese Azalea
33	7	Azalea Hinodegiri	Japanese Azalea
34	5	Spiræa arguta	Hybrid Spiræa
35	6	Kerria japonica, single	Yellow Kerria
36	12	Iris Silver King	White Flag
37	7	Hypericum Moserianum	St. John's Wort
38	6	Rosa multiflora	Dwarf Japanese Rose
39	10	Phlox divaricata	Early Blue Phlox
40	10	Aquilegia flabellata nana alba	White Columbine
41	10	Stokesia cyanea	Stokes' Aster
42	8	Iris pallida dalmatica	Lavender Flag
43	3	Pæony Festiva maxima	White Peony
44	10	Aster amellus Beauty of Ronsdorf	Michaelmas Daisy
45	12	Chrysanthemum Julia Lagravère	Red Chrysanthemum
46	3	Pæony Richardson's grandiflora	Peony
47	16	Delphinium formosum	Indigo Larkspur
48	5	Dicentra spectabilis	Bleeding Heart
49	18	Helenium Hoopesii	Early Sneezewort
50	12	Veronica longifolia subsessilis	Speedwell
51	10	Phlox Miss Lingard	Early Phlox
52	6	Kerria japonica, single	Single Kerria
53	10	Hesperis matronalis	Sweet Rocket
54	12	Chrysanthemum Golden Mme. Martha	Yellow Chrysanthemum
55	6	Weigela Eva Rathke	Dark Red Weigela
56	12	Aquilegia chrysantha	Yellow Columbine
57	8	Phlox Rheinstrom	Pink Phlox
58	8	Phlox Ardense Grete	Early White Phlox
59	5	Syringa, named varieties	Lilac
60	2	Juniperus virginiana	Red Cedar
61	9	Phlox Elizabeth Campbell	Pink Phlox
62	8	Lonicera Morrowi	Bush Honeysuckle
63	5	Hibiscus syriacus, single	Pink Rose of Sharon
64	5	Philadelphus Mont Blanc	Mock Orange

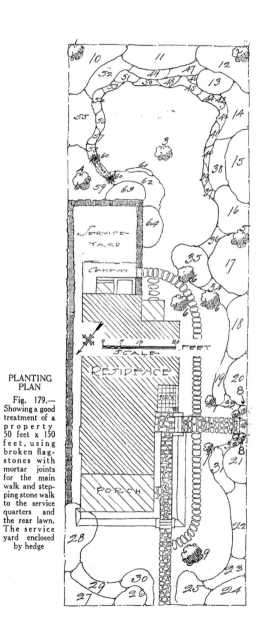

PLANTING
PLAN

Fig. 179.—
Showing a good
treatment of a
p r o p e r t y
50 feet x 150
f e e t, u s i n g
broken flag-
stones with
mortar joints
for the main
walk and step-
ping stone walk
to the service
quarters and
the rear lawn.
The service
yard enclosed
by hedge

KEY TO PLANTING PLAN.—Fig. 180

A property 75 feet x 150 feet, providing space for flower and Rose garden, tea house, pool and garage. Entrance to the garage is arranged with two cement tracks, with turf between.

Key No.	Quan.	Variety	Common Name
1	9	Juniperus virginiana	Red Cedar
2	16	Roses, Hybrid Tea (Standards)	
3	125	Hybrid Tea Roses	Everblooming Roses
4	350	Ligustrum ovalifolium	California Privet
5	3	Spiræa Van Houttei	Drooping Spiræa
6		Lonicera Morrowi $\left\{\begin{array}{l}\text{Key Nos.—6 \ 9 \ 22 \ 28 \ 38 \ 63} \\ \text{No. Plants-5 \ 5 \ 5 \ 5 \ 3 \ 3}\end{array}\right\}$	Bush Honeysuckle
7	1	Magnolia acuminata	Cucumber Tree
8	5	Viburnum Opulus sterilis	Snowball
10	10	Buddleia Veitchiana	Butterfly Plant
11	3	Biota orientalis conspicua	Columnar Chinese Arborvitæ
12	10	Desmodium japonicum	Purple Bush Clover
13	6	Hydrangea quercifolia	Oak-leaved Hydrangea
14	5	Forsythia suspensa	Drooping Golden Bell
15	1	Red Siberian Crab	Crab Apple
16	14	Dianthus barbatus	Sweet William
17		Berberis Thunbergi $\left\{\begin{array}{l}\text{Key Nos.—17 \ 18 \ 31 \ 64} \\ \text{No. Plants- 9 \ 9 \ 5 \ 7}\end{array}\right\}$	Japanese Barberry
19	6	Deutzia Lemoinei	Lemoine's Deutzia
20	8	Phlox W. C. Egan	Hardy Phlox
21	10	Iris Silver King	White Flag
23	8	Rose Pink Baby Rambler	Everblooming Rose
24	12	Rose White Baby Rambler	Everblooming Rose
25	6	Rose Hermosa	Everblooming Rose
26	8	Rose Pink Baby Rambler	Everblooming Rose
27	5	Rosa rugosa	Japanese Rose
29	3	Lonicera fragrantissima	Early Honeysuckle
30	8	Phlox Miss Lingard	Early Phlox
32	5	Juniperus Sabina	Savin Juniper
33	3	Taxus cuspidata	Japanese Yew
34	1	Larix europæa	European Larch
35	1	Cornus florida rubra	Pink Dogwood
36	2	Buxus arborescens (Globe)	Globe-shaped Box
37	4	Taxus cuspidata	Japanese Yew
39	1	Magnolia conspicua	White Magnolia
40	15	Hypericum Moserianum	St. John's Wort
41	5	Forsythia suspensa	Drooping Golden Bell
42	9	Abelia grandiflora	Hybrid Abelia
42½	7	Hydrangea radiata	Silver-leaved Hydrangea
43	8	Xanthorriza apiifolia	Yellow Root
44	6	Spiræa Thunbergii	Snow Garland
44½	4	Syringa vulgaris	Lilac
45	1	Apple, Grimes' Golden	
46	5	Philadelphus coronarius	Mock Orange
47	9	Spiræa Margaritæ	Pink Spiræa
48	3	Juniperus virginiana glauca	Blue Cedar
49	1	Liquidambar styraciflua	Sweet Gum
50	5	Hydrangea paniculata	Late Hydrangea
51	9	Œnothera missouriensis	Evening Primrose
52	10	Iris Blue Boy	German Flag
53	9	Chrysanthemum St. Illoria	Pink Chrysanthemum
54	6	Pæonia Van Houttei	Crimson Peony
55	6	Funkia cærulea	Plantain Lily
56	6	Phlox Diadem	Hardy Phlox
57	3	Pæonia festiva maxima	White Peony
58	7	Delphinium chinense	Chinese Larkspur
59	10	Iris pumila aurea	Dwarf Flag
60	8	Spiræa Thunbergii	Show Garland
61	5	Pyrus Maulei	Pink Japanese Quince
62	1	Juniperus Cannarti	Pyramidal Cedar
65	9	Phlox Eugene Danzanvilliers	Lilac Phlox
66	12	Iris aurea	Yellow Flag
67	6	Pæonia grandiflora	Pink Peony
68	12	Iris pallida dalmatica	Lavender Flag
69	8	Chrysanthemum Julia Lagravère	Red Chrysanthemum
70		Annuals and Perennials	
71	1	Populus fastigiata	Lombardy Poplar

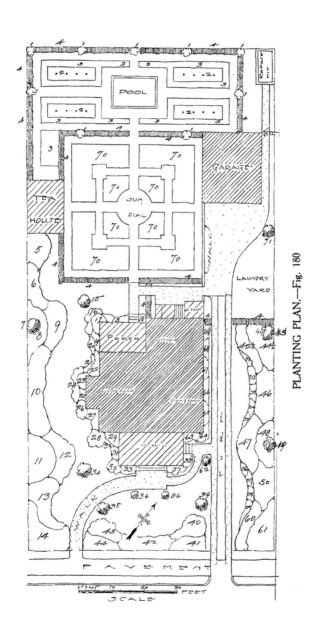

PLANTING PLAN.—Fig. 180

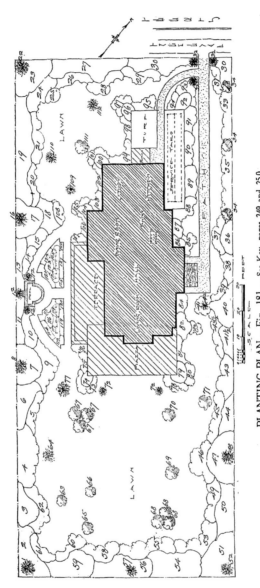

PLANTING PLAN.—Fig. 181.—See Key, pages 249 and 250

KEY TO PLANTING PLAN.—Fig. 181

A property 85 feet x 200 feet. Good arrangement for residence with kitchen wing toward the street and living-room, with a southeastern exposure, looking out on the lawn. The fountain and pool are the interesting features

Key No.	Quan.	Variety	Common Name
1	1	Pinus austriaca	Austrian Pine
2	5	Styrax japonica	Japanese Styrax
3	4	Syringa Marie Legray	White Lilac
4	8	Weigela Eva Rathke	Dark Red Weigela
5	8	Cotoneaster microphylla	Small-leaved Rose Box
6	6	Kerria japonica	Single Corchorus
7	9	Buddleia Veitchiana	Butterfly Plant
8	1	Picea orientalis	Oriental Spruce
9	12	Abelia grandiflora	Hybrid Abelia
10	8	Rhododendron Charles Dickens	Crimson Rhododendron
11	10	Rhododendron album elegans	White Rhododendron
12	3	Juniperus virginiana	Red Cedar
13	12	Rhododendron maximum roseum	Pink Rhododendron
14	7	Rhododendron Chas. Bagley	Crimson Rhododendron
15	8	Rhododendron Mrs. John Clutton	White Rhododendron
16	1	Cedrus Deodara	True Cedar
17	9	Hibiscus syriacus, single pink	Rose of Sharon
18	8	Hydrangea paniculata	Late Hydrangea
19	18	Buddleia Veitchii	Butterfly Plant
20	12	Genista tinctoria	Broom
21	11	Spiræa Thunbergii	Snow Garland
22	1	Pinus Strobus	White Pine
23	5	Cornus florida	White Dogwood
24	8	Cercis japonica	Japanese Judas
25	12	Hypericum Moserianum	St. John's Wort
26	6	Hydrangea Otaksa	Pink Large-flowering Hydrangea
27	8	Viburnum plicatum	Japanese Snowball
28	11	Spiræa A. Waterer	Dwarf Pink Spiræa
29	6	Forsythia suspensa	Drooping Golden Bell
30	7	Syringa vulgaris	Lilac
31	12	Desmodium penduliflorum	Bush Clover
32	3	Thuya Geo. Peabody	Golden Arborvitæ
33	7	Lonicera Morrowi	Japanese Bush Honeysuckle
34	3	Tilia europæa	European Linden
35	12	Rosa rubiginosa	Sweet Brier Rose
36	5	Rosa rugosa, red	Japanese Rose
37	12	Rosa, Baby Rambler white	Dwarf Everblooming Rose
38	4	Kerria japonica	Single Corchorus
39	7	Spiræa Thunbergii	Snow Garland
40	8	Buddleia Veitchiana	Butterfly Plant
41	12	Hypericum Moserianum	St. John's Wort
41½	25	Philadelphus Mont Blanc	Mock Orange
42	1	Retinispora obtusa nana	Dwarf Japanese Cedar
43	5	Weigela Eva Rathke	Dark Red Weigela
43½	10	Cotoneaster microphylla	Small-leaved Rose Box
44	5	Hydrangea quercifolia	Oak-leaved Hydrangea
45	10	Deutzia gracilis	Slender Deutzia
46	6	Hydrangea paniculata grandiflora	Large-flowering Hydrangea
47	5	Hibiscus syriacus, blue and white	Rose of Sharon
48	1	Tsuga canadensis	Hemlock
49	7	Caryopteris mastacanthus	Blue Spiræa
50	5	Lonicera fragrantissima	Fragrant Bush Honeysuckle
51	5	Cornus florida rubra	Pink Dogwood
52	1	Pinus Strobus	White Pine
53	7	Rhodotypos kerrioides	White Kerria
54	5	Weigela rosea	Pink Weigela
55	10	Spiræa Thunbergii	Snow Garland
56	7	Buddleia Veitchii	Butterfly Plant
57	1	Pseudotsuga Douglasi	Douglas Spruce
58	5	Lonicera Morrowi	Bush Honeysuckle
59	5	Syringa vulgaris	Lilac
60	7	Spiræa Thunbergii	Snow Garland
61	6	Caryopteris mastacanthus	Blue Spiræa
62	7	Forsythia suspensa	Golden Bell
63	1	Koelreuteria paniculata	Varnish Tree
64	1	Picea pungens Kosteriana	Blue Spruce

KEY TO PLANTING PLAN.—Fig. 181—Continued

Key No.	Quan.	Variety	Common Name
65	1	Larix europæa	European Linden
66	1	Magnolia Soulangeana	Pink Magnolia
67	3	Populus fastigiata	Lombardy Poplar
68	3	Betula nigra	Red Birch
69	1	Red Siberian Crab	Crab.Apple
70	1	Fraxinus americana	American Ash
71	1	Cerasus japonica rosea pendula	Weeping Cherry
72	2	Cryptomeria Lobbi compacta	Pyramidal Cryptomeria
73	10	Leucothoe Catesbæi	Pipewood
74	3	Mahonia japonica	Japanese Evergreen Barberry
75	5	Mahonia aquifolia	Holly-leaved Barberry
76	7	Azalea Hinodegiri	Evergreen Azalea
77	1	Retinispora obtusa gracilis	Thread-leaved Cedar
78	9	Leucothoe Catesbæi	Pipewood
79	4	Mahonia japonica	Japanese Evergreen Barberry
80	9	Hypericum Moserianum	St. John's Wort
81	7	Rhododendron roseum elegans	Pink Rhododendron
82	7	Rhododendron atrosanguineum	Crimson Rhododendron
83	6	Andromeda floribunda	Early Andromeda
84	5	Rhododendron maximum roseum	Pink Rhododendron
85	7	Azalea indica alba	White Azalea
86	5	Rhododendron maximum roseum	Pink Rhododendron
87	5	Rhododendron Mrs. J. Clutton	White Rhododendron
88	5	Thuya occidentalis pyramidalis	Pyramidal Arborvitæ
89	7	Cotoneaster Simonsii	Shining Rose Box
90	6	Lonicera fragrantissima	Fragrant Honeysuckle
91	7	Cotoneaster Simonsii	Shining Rose Box
92	3	Thuya occidentalis pyramidalis	Pyramidal Arborvitæ
93	8	Hydrangea paniculata grandiflora	Large-flowering Hydrangea
94	7	Desmodium penduliflorum	Bush Clover
95	5	Lonicera fragrantissima	Fragrant Bush Honeysuckle
96	3	Juniperus virginiana glauca	Blue Cedar
97	9	Spiræa A. Waterer	Dwarf Pink Spiræa
98	5	Kerria japonica fl. pl.	Double Corchorus
99	5	Viburnum plicatum	Japanese Snowball
100	3	Biota orientalis pyramidalis	Chinese Arborvitæ
101	8	Spiræa callosa rosea	Pink Spiræa
102	10	Yucca filamentosa	Adam's Needle
103	6	Buddleia Veitchii	Butterfly Plant
104	3	Juniperus virginiana	Red Cedar
105	12	Leucothoe Catesbæi	Pipewood
106	7	Mahonia aquifolia	Holly-leaved Barberry
107	5	Azalea indica alba	White Azalea
108	6	Deutzia gracilis	Slender Deutzia
109	1	Retinispora filifera	Lace-leaved Cedar
110	1	Juniperus elegantissima Leei	Golden Juniper
111	1	Salisburia adiantifolia	Maidenhair Tree
112	1	Juniperus Pfitzeriana	Pfitzer's Cedar
113	12	Phlox Ardensi Amanda	Early Phlox
114	30	Viola cornuta, purple	Tufted Pansy
115	20	Antirrhinum, yellow	Snapdragon
116	10	Iris pallida dalmatica	Lavender Flag
117	16	Phlox Von Lassburg	White Phlox
118	12	Delphinium formosum	Indigo Larkspur
119	18	Heliotrope Chieftain	Heliotrope
120	8	Geranium, white	Geranium
121	20	Antirrhinum, yellow	Snapdragon
122	30	Viola cornuta, blue	Tufted Pansy
123	8	Phlox Elizabeth Campbell	Pink Phlox
124	10	Heliopsis Pitcheriana	Orange Sunflower
125	15	Iris Kæmpferi	Japanese Iris
126	12	Phlox Ardensi Amanda	Early Phlox
127	18	Heliotrope Chieftain	Heliotrope
128	8	Geranium, white	Geranium

KEY TO PLANTING PLAN.—Fig. 182

Lot 180 feet x 240 feet. Treatment for a residence with a steep slope at the front and rear of the lot. The residence has a basement entrance with living rooms on the upper level, about ten feet above the pavement. The steep slopes are planted with shrubs and small trees of spiny or twiggy growth, affording protection without a fence or hedge, presenting a naturalistic appearance and providing a cover for birds

Key No.	Quan.	Variety	Common Name
1	15	Juniperus virginiana	Red Cedar
2	15	Spiræa Van Houttei	Drooping Spiræa
3	50	Rosa rubiginosa	Sweet Brier
4	15	Cratægus cordata	Washington Thorn
5	30	Hibiscus syriacus	Rose of Sharon
6	30	Hydrangea paniculata grandiflora	Large-flowering Hydrangea
7	12	Pæonia l'Esperance	Peony
8	20	Phlox divaricata	Early Blue Phlox
9	20	Iris Silver King	White Flag
10	35	Phlox Elizabeth Campbell	Pink Hardy Phlox
11	35	Aster grandiflorus	Michaelmas Daisy
12	15	Pæonia Van Houttei	Crimson Peony
13	40	Rudbeckia Newmani	Black-eyed Susan
14	20	Pentstemon Torreyi	Beard's Tongue
15	25	Delphinium formosum	Indigo Larkspur
16	15	Delphinium chinense	Chinese Larkspur
17	20	Funkia cærulea	Plantain Lily
18	20	Phlox Miss Lingard	Early Phlox
19	12	Dianthus barbatus	Sweet William
20	15	Delphinium elatum	Tall Blue Larkspur
21	16	Aster alpinus	Alpine Aster
22	18	Iris Mme. Chereau	German Iris
23	12	Pæonia festiva maxima	White Peony
24	30	Delphinium elatum	Tall Blue Larkspur
25	25	Rudbeckia Newmani	Black-eyed Susan
26	10	Dicentra spectabilis	Bleeding Heart
27	15	Geum coccineum	Avens
28	20	Delphinium formosum	Indigo Larkspur
29	30	Phlox Grete	Early Phlox
30	20	Iris pallida dalmatica	Lavender Flag
31	15	Funkia cærulea	Plantain Lily
32	20	Dicentra spectabilis	Bleeding Heart
33	15	Chrysanthemum Golden Queen	Hardy Chrysanthemum
34	20	Delphinium formosum	Indigo Larkspur
35	20	Aster amellus elegans	Michaelmas Daisy
36	18	Phlox Miss Lingard	Early Phlox
37	30	Iris Kæmpferi	Japanese Flag
38	30	Digitalis purpurea	Foxgloves
39	20	Doronicum plantagineum	Leopard's Bane
40	25	Scabiosa caucasica alba	White Sultan
41	20	Phlox Rheinstrom	Pink Phlox
42	30	Eupatorium cœlestinum	Hardy Ageratum
43	40	Aquilegia canadensis	Red Columbine
44	25	Helenium Hoopesii	Early Sneezewort
45	40	Digitalis purpurea	Foxgloves
46	12	Aucuba japonica, green	Japanese Laurel
47	10	Abelia grandiflora	Hybrid Abelia
48	10	Tsuga canadensis	Hemlock
	15	Tsuga canadensis	Hemlock
49	30	Cornus florida	White Dogwood
	10	Populus fastigiata	Lombardy Poplar
50	10	Tsuga canadensis	Hemlock
	26	Cratægus cordata	Washington Thorn
51	25	Syringa persica	Persian Lilac
52	40	Abelia grandiflora	Hybrid Abelia
53	20	Ligustrum Regelianum	Regel's Privet
54	12	Euonymus alatus	Cork-barked Spindle Tree
55	15	Cornus stolonifera	Red-twigged Dogwood
56	30	Stephanandra flexuosa	Stephanandra
57	30	Forsythia suspensa	Drooping Golden Bell
58	1	Abies Veitchii	Veitch's Fir

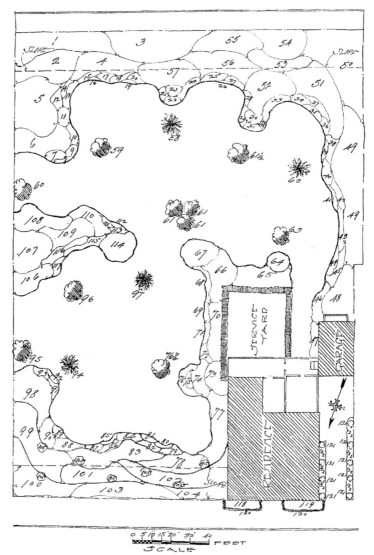

PLANTING PLAN.—Fig. 182.—Lot is 180x240 ft. See Key, pages 251 and 253

KEY TO PLANTING PLAN.—Fig. 182—Continued

Key No.	Quan.	Variety	Common Name
59	1	Betula alba	White Birch
60	1	Quercus rubra	Red Oak
61	3	Styrax japonica	Styrax
61½	1	Quercus palustris	Pin Oak
62	1	Cedrus Deodora	True Cedar
63	1	Cedrela sinensis	Chinese Cedrela
64	20	Mahonia japonica	Holly-leaved Barberry
65	40	Ligustrum lucidum	Evergreen Holly
66	12	Thuya occidentalis	Arborvitæ
67	20	Spiræa Van Houttei	Drooping Spiræa
68	25	Chrysanthemum Julia Lagravère	Dark Red Chrysanthemum
69	15	Rudbeckia Newmani	Black-eyed Susan
70	16	Lonicera fragrantissima	Early Fragrant Honeysuckle
71	18	Digitalis purpurea	Foxglove
72	15	Helianthus mollis	Sunflower
73	7	Thuya occidentalis pyramidalis	Pyramidal Arborvitæ
74	20	Spiræa A. Waterer	Dwarf Pink Spiræa
75	10	Yucca filamentosa	Adam's Needle
76	25	Hypericum Mœserianum	St. John's Wort
76½	21	Salisburia adiantifolia	Maidenhair Tree
77	20	Rhodotypos kerrioides	White Kerria
78	12	Viburnum dentatum	Arrow Wood
79	20	Heliopsis Pitcheriana	Orange Sunflower
80	10	Dicentra spectabilis	Bleeding Heart
81	20	Phlox Miss Lingard	Early Phlox
82	20	Pentstemon barbatus	Sweet William
83	40	Berberis Thunbergii	Japanese Barberry
84	30	Hesperis matronalis	Rocket
85	15	Iris aurea	Yellow Flag
86	30	Eupatorium cœlestinum	Hardy Chrysanthemum
87	15	Funkia cœrulea	Plantain Lily
88	30	Bocconia cordata	Plume Poppy
89	15	Aster lævis	Lavender Aster
90	5	Viburnum tomentosum	Japanese Snowball
91	10	Mahonia aquifolia	Holly-leaved Barberry
92	15	Hypericum Moserianum	St. John's Wort
93	20	Berberis ilicifolia	Holly-leaved Barberry
94	1	Cryptomeria japonica	Cryptomeria
95	1	Fagus sylvatica Riversi	Purple Beech
96	1	Magnolia Soulangeana	Pink Magnolia
97	1	Picea pungens Kosteriana	Blue Spruce
98	20	Magnolia glauca	Sweet Bay
99	30	Cornus stolonifera	Red-twigged Dogwood
100	60	Berberis Thunbergii	Japanese Barberry
101	50	Symphoricarpos vulgaris	Coral Berry
102	50	Rosa rubiginosa	Sweet Brier
103	50	Ligustrum Regelianum	Regel Privet
104	20	Berberis Thunbergii	Japanese Barberry
105	7	Juniperus virginiana	Red Cedar
106	8	Pyrus japonica	Japanese Quince
107	20	Exochorda grandiflora	Pearl Bush
108	25	Lonicera Morrowi	Japanese Bush Honeysuckle
109	12	Syringa vulgaris	Lilacs
110	20	Callicarpa purpurea	Beauty Berry
111	12	Pentstemon Torreyi	Beard's Tongue
112	20	Phlox divaricata	Early Blue Phlox
113	15	Hesperis matronalis	Sweet Rocket
114	100	Phlox Elizabeth Campbell	Pink Phlox
115	14	Hydrangea arborescens grandiflora alba	Hills of Snow
116	8	Hydrangea paniculata, late	Late Hydrangea
117	30	Phlox divaricata	Early Blue Phlox
118	15	Rhododendron Charles Dickens	Dark Red Rhododendron
119	15	Rhododendron roseum elegans	Pink Rhododendron
120	250	Buxus sempervirens	Box edging
121	9	Juniperus Schottii	Schott's Cedar
122	20	Rhododendron, Hybrids	Hybrid Rhododendron

KEY TO PLANTING PLAN—Fig. 183

Key No.	Quan.	Variety	Common Name
1	5	Mahonia aquifolia	Holly-leaved Barberry
2	6	Bambusa Metake	Evergreen Bamboo
3	15	Funkia caerulea	Plantain Lily
4	7	Rhododendron roseum elegans	Pink Rhododendron
5	8	Buxus (Globe Shape)	Box Bushes
6	5	Rhododendron Sargent.	Hybrid Rhododendron
7	10	Rhododendron Mrs. Milner	Hybrid Rhododendron
8	20	Funkia caerulea	Plantain Lily
8	8	Rhododendron atrosanguineum	Crimson Rhododendron
9	50	Lily of the Valley	
10	50	Ferns	
10	25	Lily of the Valley	
	30	Ferns	
		Woodland plants collected	
11	7	Populus fastigiata	Lombardy Poplar
12	16	Ligustrum Regelianum	Regel's Privet
13	2	Wistaria chinensis	Chinese Wistaria
14	2	Clematis paniculata	Japanese Clematis
15	8	Lonicera Morrowi	Bush Honeysuckle
16	2	Callicarpa purpurea	Purple Fruited Callicarpa
17	10	Spiraea prunifolium fl. pl.	Bridal Wreath
18	1	Cornus florida rubra	Red-flowering Dogwood
19	20	Hybrid Spiraea	Hybrid Spiraea
20	1	Spiraea A. Waterer	Flowering Spiraea
20	20	Fraxinus Ornus	Flowering Ash
21	1	Spiraea Van Houttei	Drooping Spiraea
22	12	Berberis Thunbergii	Japanese Barberry
23	7	Hydrangea p. g.	Large-flowering Hydrangea
24	7	Syringa Pekinensis	Chinese Lilac
25	15	Deutzia gracilis	Dwarf Deutzia
26	18	Weigela Eva Rathke	Dark Red Weigela
27	5	Cercis canadensis	Red Bud
27½	2	Catalpa speciosa	Western Catalpa
28	5	Viburnum Lantana	Wayfaring Tree
29	20	Viburnum Sieboldi	Chinese Snowball
30	2	Quercus coccinea	Scarlet Oak
31	1	Fraxinus Ornus	Flowering Ash
32	1	Picea pungens Kosteriana	Koster's Spruce
33	10	Azalea mollis, red	Japanese Azalea
34	3	Ligustrum Ibota	Ibota Privet
	3	Photinia villosa	Photinia
35	3	Sophora japonica	Japanese Sophora
36	12	Ligustrum Regelianum	Regel's Privet
37	8	Cercis japonica	Japanese Red Bud
38	20	Berberis Thunbergii	Thunberg's Barberry
39	4	Tsuga canadensis	Hemlock
40	15	Betula nigra	Red Birch
41		Symphoricarpos racemosus and vulgaris	Coral Berry and Snowberry
41	6	Vitex Agnus-Castus	Chaste Tree
42	12	Abelia grandiflora	Hybrid Abelia
43	1	Apple Maiden's Blush	Apple
44	7	Calycanthus floridus	Sweet Shrub
45	2	Spiraea Thunbergii	Snow Garland
46	5	Syringa, named varieties	Lilac
47	5	Abelia grandiflora	Hybrid Abelia
48	1	Viburnum plicatum	Japanese Snowball
49	10	Jasminum nudiflorum	Yellow Jasmine
50	12	Caryopteris mastacanthus	Blue Spiraea
51	1	Hydrangea paniculata	Late Hydrangea
52	1	Liquidambar styraciflua	Sweet Gum
53	12	Desmodium pendiliflorum	Bush Clover
54	1	Apple Smokehouse	Apple
55	1	Acer platanoides Schwedleri	Red-leaved Norway Maple
56	1	Cerasus Avium fl. pl.	White-flowering Cherry
57	1	Quercus palustris	Pin Oak
58	7	Stephanandra flexuosa	Stephanandra
59	6	Hibiscus syriacus, blue and white	Rose of Sharon
60	8	Spiraea Billardi	Pink Spiraea
61	6	Rhodotypos kerrioides	White Kerria
62	6	Kerria japonica, single	Yellow Kerria
63	1	Syringa, named kinds	Lilac
64	20	Picea pungens Kosteriana	Koster's Spruce
65	4	Viburnum tomentosum	Single Snowball
66	1	Yucca filamentosa	Adam's Needle
67	20	Spiraea A. Waterer	Dwarf Pink Spiraea
68	12	Abies balsamea	Balsam Fir
69	5	Syringa, named varieties	Lilac
70	5	Azalea mollis, yellow	Ghent Azalea
71	10	Philadelphus coronarius	Mock Orange
72	15	Salix babylonica	Willow
73	1	Lonicera fragrantissima	Fragrant Bush Honeysuckle
74	6	Syringa vulgaris alba	White Lilac
75	1	Acer polymorphum atrosanguineum	Red Japanese Maple
76	1	Quercus rubra	Red Oak
77	5	Deutzia gracilis	Slender Deutzia
78	1	Acer poly. dissectum	Cut-leaved Japanese Maple
79		Annuals	
80		Perennials	
81	10	Aster laevis	Lavender Hardy Aster
82	8	Oenothera missouriensis	Yellow Evening Primrose
83	10	Aquilegia chrysantha	Yellow Columbine
84	15	Phlox Eugene Danzanvilliers	Lavender Phlox
85	10	Iris Blue Boy	German Flag
86	10	Geum coccineum	Avens
87	8	Crataegus Oxycantha, standards	English Hawthorn
88	2	Acer saccharum	Sugar Maple

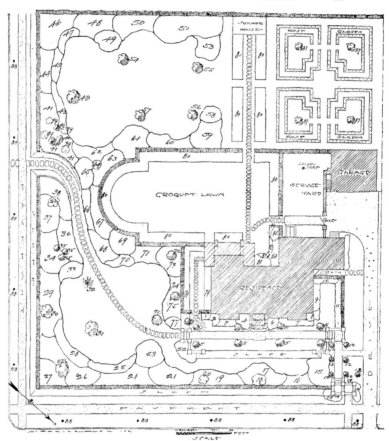

PLANTING PLAN.—Fig. 183

Fig. 183.—Lot 190 feet by 190 feet. Residence lot designed to provide a flower garden,
garage, enclosed service yard and croquet lawn. The interesting features are a
terrace walk as shown in Fig. 55, stepping stone walk in lawn as shown in
Fig. 6 and unique entrance arrangement as shown in Fig. 33

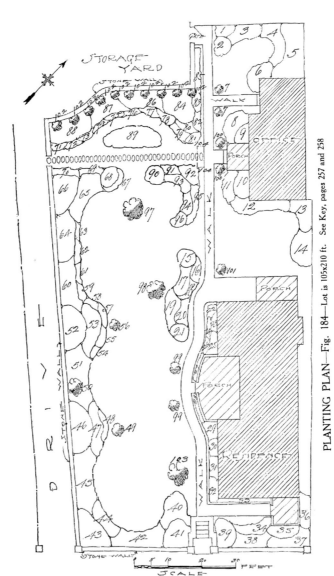

PLANTING PLAN—Fig. 184—Lot is 105x210 ft.   See Key, pages 257 and 258

KEY TO PLANTING PLAN.—Fig. 184

Arrangement designed for a contractor's residence, with detached office and good service yard arrangement

Key No.	Quan.	Variety	Common Name
1	3	Viburnum plicatum	Japanese Snowball
2	3	Forsythia suspensa	Drooping Golden Bell
3	5	Calycanthus floridus	Old-fashioned Sweet Shrub
4	6	Weigela Eva Rathke	Dark Red Weigela
5	7	Philadelphus coronarius	Mock Orange
6	6	Hydrangea p. g.	Large-flowering Hydrangea
7	2	Thuya occidentalis globosa	Globe Arborvitæ
8	9	Azalea Hinodegiri	Japanese Evergreen Azalea
9	5	Rhododendron Charles. Dickens	Hybrid Rhododendron
10	6	Rhododendron Mrs. J. Clutton	Hybrid Rhododendron
11	8	Azalea Hinodegiri	Evergreen Azalea
12	8	Rhodotypos kerrioides	White Kerria
13	4	Hibiscus syriacus, single	Pink Rose of Sharon
14	5	Hydrangea paniculata grandiflora	Large-flowering Hydrangea
15	35	Carnation (annual)	
16	25	Larkspur (annual)	
17	35	Zinnias, clear yellow	Youth and Old Age
18	12	Papaver nudicaule	Iceland Poppy
19	30	Heliotrope Chieftain	
20	15	Chrysanthemum, Shasta Daisy	Shasta Daisy
21	25	Œnothera missouriensis	Evening Primrose
22	6	Iris Mme. Chereau	White Blue Flag
23	5	Berberis Thunbergii	Japanese Barberry
24	12	Aster Alpinus	Alpine Aster
25	5	Berberis vulgaris	Common Barberry
26	8	Funkia cærulea	Plantain Lily
27	30	Begonias	
28	30	Begonias	
29	5	Abelia grandiflora	Hybrid Abelia
30	9	Funkia cærulea	Plantain Lily
31	11	Phlox Von Lasshurg	White Phlox
32	11	Chrysanthemum Shasta Daisy	
33	20	Hypericum Moserianum	St. John's Wort
34	12	Azalea amœna	Evergreen Azalea
35	8	Rhododendron roseum elegans	Hybrid Rhododendron
36	9	Rhododendron album elegans	Hybrid Rhododendron
37	11	Rhododendron Everestianum	Hybrid Rhododendron
38	9	Rhododendron, Charles Dickens	Hybrid Rhododendron
39	10	Abelia grandiflora	Hybrid Abelia
40	12	Calluna vulgaris	Scotch Heather
41	10	Abelia grandiflora	Hybrid Abelia
42	12	Spiræa A. Waterer	Dwarf Pink Spiræa
43	6	Ligustrum Regelianum	Regel's Privet
44	5	Spiræa Thunbergii	Snow Garland
45	7	Spiræa Van Houttei	Drooping Spiræa
46	6	Juniperus Schottii	Schott's Juniper
47	5	Spiræa Thunbergii	Snow Garland
48	14	Iris Yolande	Purple Flag
49	1	Cornus florida	Dogwood
50	1	Cedrela sinensis	Cedrela
51	5	Cercis japonica	Japanese Judas
52	6	Thuya occidentalis pyramidalis	Arborvitæ
53	12	Desmodium penduliflorum	Bush Clover
54	4	Pæonia Andre Lauris	Peony
55	12	Iris Kæmpferi	Japanese Iris
56	1	Cornus florida rubra	Pink Dogwood
57	14	Œnothera missouriensis	Evening Primrose
58	8	Chrysanthemum arcticum	Arctic Daisy
59	5	Pæonia Van Houttei	Peony
60	7	Buddleia Veitchiana	Butterfly Plant
61	10	Hesperis matronalis	Sweet Rocket
62	8	Hypericum Moserianum	St. John's Wort
63	8	Aquilegia canadensis	Red Columbine
64	8	Mahonia aquifolia	Holly-leaved Barberry
65	14	Deutzia gracilis	Dwarf Deutzia
66	6	Amygdalus nana, pink	Flowering Almond
67	15	Phlox divaricata	Early Blue Phlox

KEY TO PLANTING PLAN.—Fig. 184—Continued

Key No.	Quan	Variety	Common Name
68	7	Iris Silver King	White Flag
69	6	Pæonia festiva maxima	White Peony
70	8	Digitalis purpurea	Foxglove
71	8	Digitalis purpurea	Foxglove
72	8	Phlox Miss Lingard	Early Phlox
73	7	Hemerocallis flava	Yellow Day Lily
74	10	Primula polyantha	Cowslip
75	12	Iris Germanica aurea	Yellow Flag
76	10	Chrysanthemum St. Illoria	Pink Chrysanthemum
77	9	Aquilegia chrysantha	Yellow Columbine
78	8	Aster amellus elegans	Pink Aster
79	10	Funkia cærulea	Plantain Lily
80	10	Delphinium formosum	Indigo Larkspur
81	10	Delphinium chinense	Chinese Larkspur
82	10	Gaillardia grandiflora	Blanket Flower
83	8	Iris Kæmpferi	Japanese Iris
84	5	Exochorda grandiflora	Pearl Bush
85	20	Eupatorium ageratoides	Snake Root
86	6	Weigela rosea	Pink Weigela
87	6	Forsythia viridissima	Golden Bell
88	8	Hydrangea paniculata	Late Hydrangea
89	20	Hybrid Tea Roses	
90	15	Aster, Blue (annual)	
91	12	Phlox divaricata	Early Blue Phlox
92	10	Iris Kæmpferi	Japanese Iris
93	10	Phlox Elizabeth Campbell	Pink Phlox
94	8	Delphinium elatum	Hybrid Larkspur
95	25	Ageratum	
96	12	Antirrhinum, yellow	Snapdragon
97	1	Acer saccharum	Sugar Maple
98	1	Quercus palustris	Pin Oak
99	2	Acer polymorphum atropurpureum	Red Japanese Maple
100	2	Roses, standards	
101	1	Salisburia adiantifolia	Maidenhair Tree Ginkgo
102	10	Populus fastigiata	Lombardy Poplar
103	1	Tilia dasystyla	Yellow-twigged Linden
104	{ 1	Rose Tausendschon	Pink Climbing Rose
	{ 1	Rose Alberic Barbier	White Climbing Rose

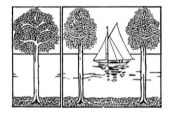

KEY TO PLANTING PLAN—Fig. 186

Fig. 186.—Treatment designed to attract birds and at the same time decrease the lawn area, thus reducing greatly the cost of maintenance

Key No.	Quan.	Variety	Common Name
1	35	Berberis Thunbergii	Japanese Barberry
2	35	Mahonia japonica	Holly-leaved Barberry
3	25	Euonymus Bungeanus	Chinese Spindle Tree
4	10	Euonymus americana	Strawberry Tree
5	17	Cerasus pennsylvanica	Honey Cherry
6	12	Viburnum Opulus sterilis	High Bush Cranberry
7	7	Cornus florida	White Dogwood
8	40	Symphoricarpos vulgaris	Coral Berry
9	20	Cotoneaster Simonsii	Shining Rose Box
10	50	Ligustrum Regelianum	Regel's Privet
11	30	Ribes aureum	Flowering Currant
	20	Itea virginica	Virginian Willow
12	50	Berberis Thunbergii	Japanese Barberry
13	60	Ligustrum Quihoui	Evergreen Privet
14	20	Cratægus Crus-galli	Shining Thorn
15	20	Photinia villosa	Photinia
16	5	Cerasus Jas. H. Veitch	Japanese Cherry
17	30	Cornus stolonifera	Red-twigged Dogwood
18	20	Eyonymus alatus	Cork-barked Spindle Tree
19	15	Lonicera tatarica	Tartarian Honeysuckle
20	35	Aralia pentaphylla	Dwarf Angelica Tree
21	35	Callicarpa purpurea	Beauty Berry
22	7	Cratægus cordata	Washington Thorn
23	30	Sambucus pubens	Red-berried Elder
24	25	Lonicera Morrowi	Japanese Bush Honeysuckle
25	35	Aralia spinosa	Hercules' Club
	30	Pinus Strobus	White Pine
26	20	Eleagnus longipes (fruiting)	Silver Thorn
26½	10	Cratægus Lelandi	Evergreen Thorn
27	75	Rhus copallina	Shining Sumach
27½	10	Lonicera Morrowi, Yellow Berried	Bush Honeysuckle
28	40	Rhus copallina	Shining Sumach
29	20	Cratægus pyracantha	Evergreen Thorn
30	5	Amelanchier botryapium	June Berry
31	30	Ilex verticillata	Deciduous Holly
32	30	Lindea benzoin	Spice Bush
33	15	Cratægus cordata	Washington Thorn
34	30	Lonicera Morrowi	Bush Honeysuckle
35	35	Pyrus arbutifolia	Choke Berry
36	35	Euonymus alatus	Cork-barked Spindle Tree
37	45	Cratægus Crus-galli	Shining Thorn
38	40	Myrica cerifera	Wax Myrtle
39	30	Ligustrum Regelianum	Regel's Privet
40	50	Viburnum dentatum	Arrow Wood
41	35	Chionanthus virginica	White Fringe
42	45	Rhodotypos kerrioides	White Kerria
43	35	Cornus alternifolia	Blue Dogwood
44	65	Symphoricarpos vulgaris	Coral Berry
45	45	Viburnum cassinoides	Withe Rod
46	50	Ilex glabra	Inkberry
47	40	Viburnum Lantana	Wayfaring Tree
48	15	Cratægus Oxycantha	English Hawthorn
49	40	Cornus sibirica	Red-twigged Cornel
50	25	Pinus rigida	Pitch Pine
51	25	Viburnum prunifolium	Sheep Berry
52	18	Rhamnus caroliniensis	Buckthorn
53	15	Pinus Mughus	Dwarf Pine
54	30	Cornus paniculata	Panicled Dogwood
55	20	Berberis Thunbergii	Japanese Barberry
	30	Berberis vulgaris	Common Barberry
56	20	Cornus florida	White Dogwood
57	30	Cornus mascula	Cornelian Cherry
58	50	Viburnum dilitatum	Japanese Bush Cranberry
59	14	Lonicera Ruprechtiana	Bush Honeysuckle
60	40	Tsuga canadensis	Hemlock Spruce
61	20	Cornus florida	White Dogwood
62	25	Eleagnus longipes	Silver Thorn

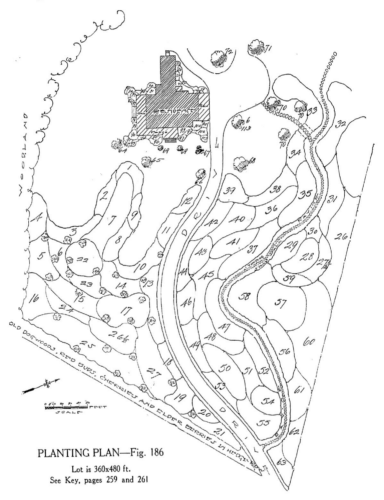

PLANTING PLAN—Fig. 186

Lot is 360x480 ft.
See Key, pages 259 and 261

KEY TO PLANTING PLAN—Fig. 186—Continued

Key No.	Quan.	Variety	Common Name
63	50	Symphoricarpus racemosus	Snowberry
64	1	Ulmus americana	American Elm
65	1	Tilia americana	American Linden
66	1	Acer saccharum	Sugar Maple
67	3	Populus fastigiata	Lombardy Poplar
68	2	Quercus palustris	Pin Oak
69	2	Buxus arborescens, untrimmed	Old-fashioned Box
70	3	Quercus coccinea	Scarlet Oak
71	1	Quercus rubra	Red Oak
72	1	Quercus rubra	Red Oak
73	7	Rhododendron Charles Dickens	Hybrid Rhododendron
74	7	Azalea indica alba	White Azalea
75	7	Rhododendron Mrs. J. Clutton	White Rhododendron
76	12	Abelia grandiflora	Hybrid Abelia
77	12	Rhododendron album elegans	Hybrid Rhododendron
78	5	Rhododendron Charles Dickens	Hybrid Rhododendron
79	7	Azalea Hinodegiri	Evergreen Azalea
80	10	Abelia grandiflora	Hybrid Abelia
81	8	Rhododendron album elegans	White Rhododendron
82	8	Rhododendron John Waterer	Hybrid Rhododendron
83	9	Rhododendron roseum elegans	Hybrid Rhododendron
84	14	Azalea Hinodegiri	Evergreen Azalea
85	14	Hypericum Moserianum	St. John's Wort
86	6	Azalea indica alba	White Azalea
87	5	Aucuba japonica, green	Japanese Laurel
88	8	Abelia grandiflora	Hybrid Abelia
89	6	Spiræa Thunbergii	Snow Garland
90	7	Lonicera Morrowi	Bush Honeysuckle
91	12	Phlox Elizabeth Campbell	Pink Hardy Phlox
92	8	Phlox Grete	Early Phlox
93	12	Iris Silver King	White Flag
94	12	Pæonia Andre Lauris	Red Peony
95	6	Buddleia Veitchii	Butterfly Shrub
96	14	Phlox Von Lassburg	White Phlox
97	10	Phlox Eugene Danzanvilliers	Mauve Phlox
98	7	Kerria japonica, single	Yellow Kerria
99	10	Chrysanthemum Golden Mme. Martha	Yellow Chrysanthemum
100	7	Rhodotypos kerrioides	White Kerria
101	10	Funkia cærulea	Plantain Lily
102	12	Pentstemon Torreyi	Beard's Tongue
103	8	Dianthus barbatus, white	Sweet William
104	5	Morus tatarica	Russian Mulberry
105	6	Quercus rubra	Red Oak
106	2	Cerasus pennsylvanica	Wild Cherry
107	2	Prunus serotina	Wild Black Cherry
108	1	Quercus tinctoria	Black Oak
109	2	Larix europæa	European Larch
110	2	Kœlreuteria paniculata	Varnish Tree
111	3	Pyrus americana	Mountain Ash
112	3	Magnolia acuminata	Cucumber Tree
113	1	Quercus palustris	Pin Oak

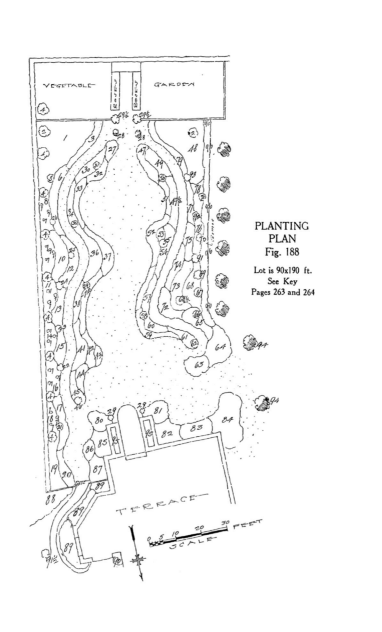

PLANTING
PLAN
Fig. 188

Lot is 90x190 ft.
See Key
Pages 263 and 264

KEY TO PLANTING PLAN.— Fig. 188

Unusual flower garden, designed on informal lines, planted with perennials and annuals to provide an abundance of bloom in masses throughout the Summer

Key No.	Quan.	Variety	Common Name
1	3	Forsythia viridissima	Golden Bell
	3	Philadelphus coronarius	Mock Orange
	3	Hydrangea paniculata, late	Late Hydrangea
2	2	Populus Bolleana	Silver-leaved Pyramidal Poplar
3	25	Arabis albida	Rock Cress
	50	Narcissus Von Sion	Daffodil
4	9	Juniperus virginiana	Red Cedar
5	1	Juniperus Schottii	Pyramidal Juniper
6	50	Iris pallida dalmatica	Lavender Flag
7	18	Syringa, named kinds	Lilacs
8	20	Lilium auratum	Gold Banded Lily
9	8	Rudbeckia laciniata fl. pl.	Golden Glow
10	37	Delphinium hybridum	Larkspur
11	8	Aster novi-belgii, var. Climax	Lavender Blue Hardy Aster
12	30	Chrysanthemum Boston	Yellow Chrysanthemum
13	30	Marigolds	
14	9	Centaurea montana	Cornflower
15	15	Campanula persicifolia	Peach-leaved Bellflower
16	9	Pæonia, named kinds	
17	30	Houstonia serpyllifolia	Bluets
	30	Pansies	
18	20	Lilium speciosum roseum	Japanese Lilies
19	25	Digitalis purpurea	Foxglove
20	15	Eupatorium cælestinum	Hardy Ageratum
21	1	Juniperus Cannarti	Pyramidal Juniper
22	1	Juniperus chinensis	Chinese Pyramidal Juniper
23	1	Juniperus Schottii	Pyramidal Cedar
24	1	Juniperus Cannarti	Pyramidal Cedar
25	1	Juniperus virginiana glauca	Pyramidal Cedar
26	1	Juniperus chinensis	Pyramidal Cedar
27	18	Marigolds	
28	2	Juniperus Cannarti	Pyramidal Cedar
29	2	Juniperus Cannarti	Pyramidal Cedar
29½	2	Ligustrum ovalifolium (to form an arch)	California Privet
30	20	Gladiolus Sulphur King	Yellow Gladiolus
	20	Pæonia edulis superba	Pink Peony
31	1	Biota orientalis conspicua	Oriental Arborvitæ
32	20	Mignonette	
33	30	Delphinium (annual)	Larkspur
34	27	Phlox Elizabeth Campbell	Pink Phlox
35	1	Thuya plicata	Fern-leaved Arborvitæ
36	45	Phlox, Miss Lingard	Early White Phlox
37	40	Heliotrope	
38	20	Shasta Daisy	
39	1	Cryptomeria japonica	
40	40	Ageratum	
41	40	Zinnias, salmon pink	
42	27	Campanula latifolia macrantha	Bellflower
43	20	Clarkia	
44	30	Viola lutea splendens	Tufted Pansy
45	25	China Asters, pink	
46	1	Retinispora obtusa nana	Dwarf Japanese Cypress
47	40	Ageratum	
47½	40	Zinnias, clear yellow	
48	3	Forsythia viridissima	Golden Bell
	3	Exorchorda grandiflora	Pearl Bush
	3	Hydrangea paniculata, late	Late Hydrangea
49	45	Phlox, Mrs. Jenkins	White Phlox
50	1	Cryptomeria japonica	
51	45	Iberis sempervirens	Candytuft
52	65	Scabiosa (Pansies along edge)	Blue Bonnet
53	5	Papaver orientale	Oriental Poppy
54	48	Phlox Rheinlander	Salmon Pink Phlox
55	1	Biota orientalis conspicua	Oriental Arborvitæ
56	45	Viola cornuta purpurea	Tufted Pansy

KEY TO PLANTING PLAN.—Fig. 188—Continued

Key No.	Quan.	Variety	Common Name
57	27	Chrysanthemum Thode	Pink Chrysanthemum
58	1	Juniperus chinensis	Chinese Pyramidal Juniper
59	50	Pink Petunias	
60	26	Phlox W. C. Egan	Hardy Phlox
61	30	Lupinus polyphyllus	Lupines
62	1	Thuya plicata	Fern-leaved Arborvitæ
63	25	Gladiolus America	Pink Gladiolus
	15	Pæonia Andre Lauris	Deep Pink Peony
64	15	Mallow Marvels (sow 1 pkg. of Sweet Alyssum seed as cover)	
65	6	Buddleia Veitchiana	Butterfly Shrub
	16	Aquilegia cærulea	Columbine Blue
66	1	Syringa Marie LeGraye	Lilac, White
67	1	Syringa Charles X	Lilac, Red
68	20	Boltonia asteroides	Starwort
68½	1	Syringa Josikæa	Hungarian Lilac
69	1	Juniperus Cannarti	Pyramidal Juniper
70	1	Syringa Mme. Lemoine	Lilac, White
71	1	Cornus florida rubra	Pink Dogwood
72	20	Pansies around edge	
	25	Pæonia festiva maxima	White Peony
73	40	Delphinium hybridum	Larkspur
74	25	Lilium candidum	Madonna Lily
75	27	Salpiglossis	
76	18	Dahlias, Cactus varieties	
77	30	Phlox Frau Anton Buchner	Hardy Phlox
78	17	Hollyhocks, pink	
79	50	Narcissus (under shrubbery)	
	50	Viola White Perfection	Tufted Pansy
80	5	Juniperus squamata	Spreading Juniper
81	5	Juniperus squamata	Spreading Juniper
82	5	Juniperus Sabina	Savin's Spreading Juniper
83	5	Juniperus Sabina tamaricifolia	Savin's Tamarix-leaved
84	5	Juniperus tripartita	Juniper
85	5	Taxus canadensis	American Yew
86	3	Taxus canadensis	American Yew
87	1	Tsuga canadensis	Hemlock Spruce
88	15	Berberis Thunbergii	Japanese Barberry
89	9	Rhododendrons, hybrid	
90	1	Rhododendrons, hybrid	
91	1	Cornus florida	White Dogwood
91½	1	Tsuga Sargent's Weeping	Weeping Hemlock
92	1	Syringa, named variety	Lilac
93	1	Syringa, named variety	Lilac
94	2	Cerasus rosea pendula	Japanese Weeping Cherry
95	100	Vinca rosea alba	White Madagascar Periwinkle
96	50	Dwarf Pink Cosmos	

KEY TO PLANTING PLAN—Fig. 190

A good walk arrangement and planting treatment for a church property. Such properties are often devoid of any such planting, which detracts greatly from the general appearance.

Key No.	Quan.	Variety	Common Name
1	16	Quercus rubra	Red Oak
2	10	Mahonia japonica	Japanese Mahonia
3	30	Leucothoe Catesbæi	Drooping Andromeda
4	20	Yucca filamentosa	Adam's Needle
5	5	Lonicera Standishi	Standish's Bush Honeysuckle
6	10	Lonicera Morrowi	Japanese Bush Honeysuckle
7	7	Rhodotypos kerrioides	White Kerria
8	1	Quercus palustris	Pin Oak
9	1	Quercus coccinea	Scarlet Oak
10	5	Juniperus Schottii	Schott's Juniper
11	12	Azalea amœna	Hardy Evergreen Azalea
12	1	Quercus tinctoria	Black Oak
13	15	Leucothoe Catesbæi	Catesby's Leucothoe
14	7	Lonicera Standishi	Standish's Bush Honeysuckle
15	7	Rhodotypos kerrioides	White Kerria
16	8	Aucuba japonica, green	Japanese Laurel
17	12	Leucothoe Catesbæi	Catesby's Leucothoe
18	6	Mahonia japonica	Japanese Mahonia
19	9	Mahonia aquifolia	Oregon Barberry
20	3	Thuya plicata	Fern-leaved Arborvitæ
21	5	Taxus canadensis	Canadian Yew
22	7	Taxus cuspidata	Japanese Yew
23	10	Leucothoe Catesbæi	Catesby's Leucothoe
24	5	Juniperus virginiana	Red Cedar
25	5	Juniperus tamariscifolia	Tamarix-leaved Juniper
26	8	Cotoneaster horizontalis	Prostrate Cotoneaster
27	5	Biota orientalis	Oriental Arborvitæ
28	5	Taxus baccata	English Yew
29	1	Juniperus Cannarti	Pyramidal Juniper
	4	Ilex crenata	Japanese Holly
30	8	Cotoneaster microphylla	Small-leaved Cotoneaster
31	8	Cotoneaster microphylla	Small-leaved Cotoneaster
32	1	Juniperus Cannarti	Pyramidal Cedar
	5	Ilex crenata	Japanese Holly
33	5	Taxus baccata	English Yew
34	1	Juniperus Cannarti	Pyramidal Cedar
	5	Ilex crenata	Japanese Holly
35	1	Juniperus Cannarti	Pyramidal Cedar
	5	Ilex crenata	Japanese Holly
36	8	Abelia grandiflora	Hybrid Abelia
37	5	Taxus cuspidata	Japanese Yew
38	1	Juniperus Cannarti	Pyramidal Cedar
	3	Ilex crenata	Japanese Holly
39	1	Juniperus Cannarti	Pyramidal Cedar
	4	Ilex crenata	Japanese Holly
40	12	Abelia grandiflora	Hybrid Abelia
41	12	Abelia grandiflora	Hybrid Abelia
42	8	Mahonia aquifolia	Oregon Barberry
43	5	Lonicera fragrantissima	Fragrant Bush Honeysuckle
44	15	Leucothoe Catesbæi	Catesby's Leucothoe
45	4	Cotoneaster Simonsii	Shining-leaved Rose Box
46	8	Bambusa Metake	Japanese Cane
47	10	Abelia grandiflora	Hybrid Abelia
48	5	Azalea Hinodegiri	Evergreen Azalea
49	7	Weigela Eva Rathke	Dark Red Weigela
50	7	Deutzia gracilis	Slender Deutzia
51	12	Lonicera Morrowi	Japanese Bush Honeysuckle
52	5	Hydrangea p. g.	Large-flowered Hydrangea
53	7	Hibiscus, single pink	Rose of Sharon
54	10	Hydrangea arborescens g. a.	" Hills of Snow "
55	7	Hibiscus, single pink	Rose of Sharon
56	10	Ligustrum Regelianum	Regel's Privet
57	9	Cotoneaster Simonsii	Shining-leaved Rose Box
58	480	Ligustrum ovalifolium	California Privet
59	1	Ulmus Americana	American Elm

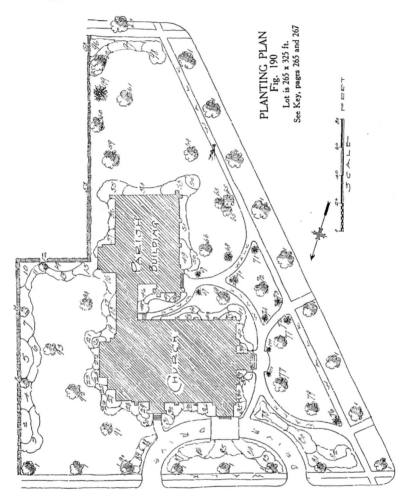

PLANTING PLAN
Fig. 190
Lot is 265 x 325 ft.
See Key, pages 265 and 267

KEY TO PLANTING PLAN.—Fig. 190—Continued

Key No.	Quan.	Variety	Common Name
60	1	Cerasus avium fl. pl.	European Double-flowered Cherry
61	1	Salisburia adiantifolia	Maidenhair Tree (Ginkgo)
62	1	Salisburia adiantifolia	Maidenhair Tree (Ginkgo)
63	1	Quercus rubra	Red Oak
64	1	Acer saccharum	Silver Maple
65	3	Cratægus Oxycantha, pink	May Thorn
66	1	Retinispora obtusa nana	Japanese Cypress
67	2	Biota orientalis compacta	Compact Oriental Arborvitæ
68	1	Cedrus Libani	Cedar of Lebanon
69	1	Salisburia adiantifolia	Maidenhair Tree (Ginkgo)
70	1	Taxus baccata	English Yew
71	1	Buxus arborescens pyramidalis	Pyramidal Box
72	1	Larix europæa	European Larch
73	1	Buxus arborescens pyramidalis	Pyramidal Box
74	1	Taxus baccata	English Yew
75	3	Juniperus virginiana	Red Cedar
76	2	Buxus arborescens pyramidalis	Pyramidal Box
77	2	Larix europæa	European Larch
78	15	Berberis Thunbergii	Thunberg's Barberry
79	1	Fagus Riversi	River's Purple Beech
80	15	Yucca filamentosa	Adams' Needle
81	12	Ligustrum Regelianum	Regel's Privet
82	12	Spiræa A. Waterer	Dwarf Pink Spiræa
83	15	Rhododendron Mrs. J. Clutton	Hybrid Rhododendron
84	15	Rhododendron Charles Dickens	Hybrid Rhododendron
85	15	Rhododendron Album elegans	Hybrid Rhododendron
86	15	Rhododendron Charles Dickens	Hybrid Rhododendron
87	10	Rhododendron roseum elegans	Hybrid Rhododendron
88	7	Ligustrum Regelianum	Regel's Privet
89	8	Berberis Thunbergii	Thunberg's Barberry
90	12	Hypericum Moserianum	St. John's Wort
91	1	Acer platanoides Schwedleri	Schwedler's Purple Maple
92	1	Salisburia adiantifolia	Maidenhair Tree (Ginkgo)
93	1	Liquidambar styraciflua	Sweet Gum
94	1	Cornus florida rubra	Pink Dogwood
95	6	Caryopteris mastacanthus	Verbena Shrub
96	4	Philadelphus Lemoinei	Lemoine's Monkshood
97	9	Ligustrum Regelianum	Regel's Privet
98	12	Berberis Thunbergii	Japanese Barberry

KEY TO PLANTING PLAN.—Fig. 187

Treatment for the space between residence, and garage and servants' quarters. Plantings designed to conceal the approach to the servants' quarters from the lawn proper and provide an interesting walk to the vegetable garden

Key No.	Quan.	Variety	Common Name
1	13	Juniperus virginiana	Red Cedar
2	1	Populus fastigiata	Lombardy Poplar
3	4	Lonicera fragrantissima	Fragrant Honeysuckle
4	8	Lonicera Morrowi	Bush Honeysuckle
		Lonicera fragrantissima	Fragrant Honeysuckle

Key No.—5 7 14 44 56 64
Quantity—3 7 18 12 20 6

Key No.	Quan.	Variety	Common Name
6	8	Lonicera Morrowi	Bush Honeysuckle
8	7	Forsythia suspensa	Drooping Golden Bell
8	7	Syringa persica	Persian Lilac
9	2	Philadelphus Lemoinei	Lemoine's Mock Orange
10	12	Caryopteris mastacanthus	Verbena Shrub
11	7	Kerria japonica, single	Single Yellow Kerria
12	14	Ligustrum amurense	Amoor River Privet
13	15	Ligustrum Regelianum	Regel's Privet
15	20	Rosa humilis	Wild Rose
16	12	Spiraea tomentosa	Pink Spirea
17	11	Vaccinium corymbosum	Blue Berry
18	10	Rosa rugosa	Japanese Rose
19	25	Rosa blanda	Wild Rose
20		Acer saccharum	Sugar Maple
21		Quercus rubra	Red Oak
22	1	Magnolia Fraseri	Fraser's Magnolia
23	20	Caryopteris mastacanthus	Verbena Shrub
24	8	Syringa vulgaris	Lilac
25	25	Buddleia Veitchiana	Butterfly Plant
26	10	Weigela rosea	Pink Weigela
27	20	Abelia grandiflora	Hybrid Abelia
28	15	Buddleia Veitchiana	Butterfly Plant
29	15	Jasminum nudiflorum	Yellow Jasmine
30	15	Cotoneaster Simonsi	Shining Rose Box
31	15	Lonicera Morrowi	Bush Honeysuckle
33	12	Deutzia gracilis	Dwarf Deutzia
34	20	Spiraea A. Waterer	Dwarf Pink Spirea
35	15	Rhodotypos kerrioides	White Kerria
36	8	Hydrangea paniculata	Late Hydrangea

Key No.	Quan.	Variety	Common Name
37	15	Rosa rugosa	Japanese Rose
38	8	Philadelphus coronarius	Mock Orange
39	20	Kerria japonica, single	Yellow Kerria
40	12	Syringa vulgaris	Lilac
41	40	Buddleia Veitchiana	Butterfly Plant
42	12	Ligustrum amurense	Amoor River Privet
43	12	Philadelphus grandiflorus	Mock Orange
45	8	Weigela rosea	Pink Weigela
46	15	Weigela Eva Rathke	Red Weigela
47	10	Spiraea Thunbergii	Snow Garland
48	9	Jasminum nudiflorum	Yellow Jasmine
49	9	Spiraea Douglasi	Pink Spirea
50	10	Berberis Thunbergii	Japanese Barberry
51	8	Berberis Thunbergii	Japanese Barberry
52	8	Jasminum nudiflorum	Yellow Jasmine
53	8	Hydrangea pan. grand.	Large-flowering Hydrangea
54	6	Althea, single pink	Rose of Sharon
55	25	Cornus sericea	Silky Cornel
57	12	Viburnum acerifolium	Maple-leaved Viburnum
58	20	Vaccinium corymbosum	Blue Berry
59	30	Azalea viscosa	Sweet Wild Honeysuckle
60	18	Rubus odoratus	Flowering Bramble
61	20	Hydrangea arborescens	Native Hydrangea
62	8	Viburnum lantanoides	Hobble Bush
63	20	Abelia grandiflora	Hybrid Abelia
65	1	Magnolia acuminata	Cucumber Tree
66	1	Magnolia tripetala	Large-leaved Magnolia
67	5	Populus fastigiata	Lombardy Poplar
68	162	Ligustrum amurense	Amoor River Privet
69	8	Rhus copallina	Shining Sumach
70	1	Juniperus Hibernica	Irish Juniper
71	50	Abelia grandiflora	Hybrid Abelia
72	1	Fraxinus americana	American Ash
73	1	Quercus tinctoria	Black Oak
74	1	Quercus imbricaria	Shingle Oak

Including driveway
lot is 217x300 ft.

PLANTING
PLAN
Fig. 187

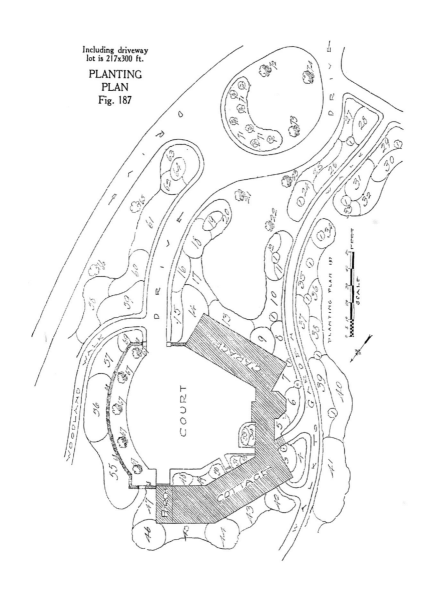

KEY TO PLANTING PLAN.—Fig. 185

Key No.	Quan.	Variety	Common Name
1	20	Hypericum Moserianum	St. John's Wort
2	5	Azalea indica alba	Hardy White Azalea
3	15	Rhododendron hybrids	Hybrid Rhododendron
4	2	Buxus arborescens (untrimmed)	Old-fashioned Box
5	15	Rhododendron hybrids	Hybrid Rhododendron
6	6	Azalea indica alba	Hardy White Azalea
7	20	Hypericum Moserianum	St. John's Wort
8	5	Lonicera Morrowi	Bush Honeysuckle
9	4	Hydrangea paniculata	Late Hydrangea
10	4	Abelia grandiflora	Hybrid Abelia
11	6	Azalea Hinodegiri	Evergreen Azalea
12	2	Tilia dasystyla	Crimean Linden
13	5	Hibiscus, single pink	Rose of Sharon
14	5	Hydrangea arborescens grandiflora alba	Everblooming Hydrangea
15	7	Spiræa arguta	Hybrid Spiræa
16	5	Philadelphus Lemoinei	Mock Orange
17	10	Rosa Baby Rambler	Baby Rambler Rose
18	6	Weigela Eva Rathke	Dark Red Weigela
19	7	Deutzia gracilis	Slender Deutzia
20	6	Hydrangea paniculata	Late Hydrangea
21	12	Mahonia aquifolia	Holly-leaved Barberry
22	18	Pachysandra terminalis	Pachysandra
23	18	Hypericum Moserianum	St. John's Wort
24	9	Stephanandra flexuosa	Stephanandra
25	3	Hydrangea paniculata, early	Hydrangea
26	5	Weigela Eva Rathke	Dark Red Weigela
27	8	Buddleia Veitchii	Butterfly Plant
28	7	Spiræa Thunbergii	Snow Garland
29	7	Spiræa callosa alba	Dwarf White Spiræa
30	4	Viburnum plicatum	Japanese Snowball
31	8	Desmodium penduliflorum	Bush Clover
32	9	Abelia grandiflora	Hybrid Abelia
33	7	Lonicera Morrowi	Bush Honeysuckle
34	8	Azalea indica alba	White Azalea
35	15	Vinca minor	Periwinkle
36		Annuals and Bulbs	
37	1000	Buxus suffruticosa	Dwarf Box
38	2	Acer polymorphum ampelopsilobum	Japanese Maple
39	6	Cotoneaster horizontalis	Trailing Rose Box

PLANTING PLAN.—Fig. 185
Lot is 127x150 ft.

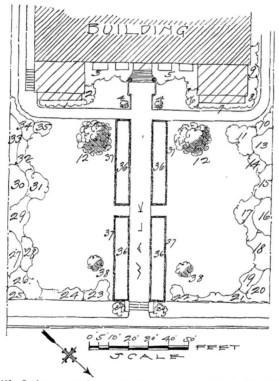

Fig. 185.—Good arrangement for a straight, Box-bordered approach to school, hospital or institutional building

PLANTING PLAN.—Fig. 189

Lot is 66x180 ft.

KEY TO PLANTING PLAN —Fig. 189

Treatment to provide a picturesque setting for a public monument. The appearance of many such features would be enhanced by a somewhat similar planting arrangement

Key No.	Quan.	Variety	Common Name
1	25	Berberis Thunbergii	Japanese Barberry
2	5	Abelia grandiflora	Hybrid Abelia
3	5	Viburnum molle	Viburnum
4	5	Abelia grandiflora	Hybrid Abelia
5	5	Viburnum molle	Viburnum
6	5	Abelia grandiflora	Hybrid Abelia
7	5	Viburnum molle	Viburnum
8	5	Abelia grandiflora	Hybrid Abelia
9	5	Viburnum molle	Viburnum
10	5	Abelia grandiflora	Hybrid Abelia
11	7	Cerasus Laurocerasus	English Laurel
12	10	Juniperus virginiana	Red Cedar
13	7	Biota orientalis compacta	Chinese Arborvitæ
14	30	Yucca filamentosa	Adams' Needle
15	4	Ilex crenata	Japense Holly
16	10	Berberis Thunbergii	Japanese Barberry
17	40	Berberis Thunbergii	Japanese Barberry
18	4	Buxus pyramidalis	Pyramid Box
19	2	Ulmus americana	American Elm

GLOSSARY OF TECHNICAL TERMS

Axis—A line actually drawn and used as the basis of measurement.

Bar Sand—Seashore sand.

Batter (or break back)—A term used to signify a wall or other material which does not stand upright but inclines from you when you stand before it.

Breaker Dust—The finest material from the stone crusher.

Broad Mortar Joint—Mortar joint from one-half to three-quarters of an inch in brick, and from one to two inches in stone work.

Cheek Block: Cheek Walls—The walls at the ends of steps, into which the steps are built.

Forebay—A small reservoir or receiving basin at the head of a pipe leading to a ram or pump.

Laid Quarry Face (Stone)—The natural rock face of the stone as taken from the quarry.

Napping Hammer—Long-handled hammer used in breaking stone, weighing four to six pounds.

Neat Width—Exact width.

Ramp—A concavity in a wall or railing rising from a lower to a higher level, or descending from a higher to a lower level.

Reveal Joint—Unpointed joints between the stones forming a wall, the mortar being raked out with a small tool from two to three inches deep.

Row-lock Fashion—Brick laid on edge as a coping or cover on top of a wall.

Rubble Gutter and Curb—Undressed stone from the field or quarry, laid at random.

Scotched Wall—Stone set on edge; that is, the narrow way up, and one stone rising above the other alternately.

Splint Spawls—The small stone resulting from dressing stone at the quarry; pieces which are too small for building purposes.

Template—A mould used for forming or setting work.

INDEX TO CONTENTS

INDEX TO CONTENTS—Continued

LaVergne, TN USA
10 January 2010
169500LV00003B/61/P